ROUNDERS

The Skills of the Game

THE • SKILLS • OF • THE • GAME

ROUNDERS

Alison Leslie
and Liz Cummins

The Crowood Press

First published in 1999 by
The Crowood Press Ltd
Ramsbury, Marlborough
Wiltshire SN8 2HR

British Library Cataloguing-in-Publication Data

A catalogue record for this book is available from the British Library.

ISBN 1 86126 234 5

Acknowledgements
Photographs by Graham Cox of Keinton Mandeville. Cover photographs and Figs 5, 11, 21, 22, 37, 42, 52, 110, 121 and 149 supplied by Ian Dixon. Figs 15, 123, 128, 129 and 157 supplied by Jamie Randall.

Thanks to the National Rounders Association, Millfield Preparatory School and Port Regis School.

Typeset by Phoenix Typesetting, Ilkley, West Yorkshire

Printed and bound by WBC Book Manufacturers, Mid Glamorgan

Contents

Alison Leslie.

Liz Cummins.

Alison Leslie has been involved in rounders as a player, coach and umpire for twenty-five years and in 1997 she was appointed coach to the England U14 squad. She is a chartered physiotherapist with coaching and umpiring qualifications in rounders, hockey and netball, and is a member of the National Association of Sports Coaches. At present she is coaching at Port Regis School, Dorset and Buckler's Mead Community School, Somerset.

Liz Cummins has a degree in Sports Science and a PGCE. She has been a teacher for fourteen years and is currently teaching at Millfield Preparatory School, Somerset. Liz has coaching and umpiring qualifications in rounders, netball and lacrosse, and has been coaching the U14 England Rounders Team with Alison Leslie.

For a long time rounders has been the sport for all, enjoyed by many but understood by few! This book is the best guide yet to achieving excellence, confirming Alison Leslie and Liz Cummins' standing as coaches of the highest standard.

Without doubt this book is an excellent read and it is sure to improve the performance of school, club or social players, and those aspiring to international honours.

Mark Linfitt
England Team Manager

Rounders – The Skills of the Game is a must for those people wishing to take the game to a higher level. Alison and Liz use their extensive experience at local and national level to improve the tactical awareness of the reader.

With the growth in popularity of the game, this book is a welcome addition and meets an increasing demand for knowledge of the higher order skills of rounders.

By careful application of the recommended practices more coaches will be able to prepare their teams for county and national tournaments.

Brian Mackinney
National Development Officer, National Rounders Association

Introduction

Rounders is a fast, exciting game which provides players with the opportunity to develop running, batting, bowling and fielding skills. It may be played by single-sex or mixed teams and, as it is a non-contact game, players of all ages and abilities may participate safely. Rounders is suitable for those with learning or physical disabilities and the rules, equipment and pitch markings may easily be adapted for these groups if necessary.

Rounders is played extensively in schools and support for the game is rapidly growing with the spread of adult leagues around the country. National representation is well established and England teams are selected at satellite coaching centres around the country. It is now possible for players to represent England, Wales or Scotland from the age of twelve upwards, with teams in each age group up to senior level.

Participation in rounders is socially rewarding and the game fosters great team spirit. Skills developed in rounders may be extended to other games involving striking, such as cricket and baseball, and also to other sports, particularly athletics and tennis.

THE NATIONAL ROUNDERS ASSOCIATION

The National Rounders Association (NRA) was formed in 1943 as the governing body for the game. It is supported by the Sports Council and is responsible for the running of rounders throughout the country and the implementation of the national rules. Encouragement and support are provided by the NRA for players of all abilities and advice in starting up and running leagues is available.

Membership of the NRA may be individual or through a club, a youth club, a school, a school association or the national body. All regular players are encouraged to join. Associate membership is also available to league players. There are many benefits of full membership of the NRA, including access to coaching and umpiring courses, voting rights, entry to NRA tournaments, club insurance and discounts on equipment and publications. Players who wish to be considered for national selection must be members of the NRA. All enquiries about membership, coaching, umpiring, tournaments and the NRA Awards Scheme for Schools should be addressed to:

The National Rounders Association
  National Office,
38 Hardy Street, Kimberley,
  Nottingham NG16 2JX
(telephone: 0115 9385478
  website: rounders@punters.co.uk)
  All the technical terms used in the book are in italics on their first appearance and are explained in the Glossary. To avoid any confusion, skills have been described for the right-handed player and may be reversed where necessary.

The key on this page indicates the symbols used throughout this book.

⊙	post
●	cone
✕	batter
▲	fielder
△	previous position of fielder
······►	path of ball
− − −►	path of player
U	umpire
○	hoop / chalk circle

1
The Game

THE FORMAT OF THE GAME

Rounders is played by two teams of nine players from a squad of up to fifteen, on a pitch marked out as shown (*Fig 1*). For some matches the pitch markings may include a *boundary line* in the forward area, measured from the front right-hand corner of the *batting square* and extending for 50m (40m up to and including under-fourteen players).

THE AIM

The aim of the game is to score more *rounders* than the other team within the duration of the *innings*. The team who are in to bat try to score as many rounders as possible by hitting the ball at the most effective height, angle and distance to allow the unchecked progression of the batter around the track to the fourth post. An innings may be of a fixed, timed

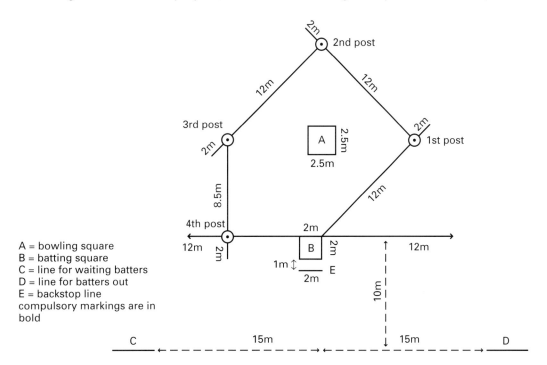

A = bowling square
B = batting square
C = line for waiting batters
D = line for batters out
E = backstop line
compulsory markings are in
bold

Fig 1 Dimensions of the pitch.

period, a certain number of *good balls* or until the batting team are all out. Both teams receive the same amount of time or number of good balls, provided that they remain in. There are normally two innings for each side. As soon as a winning score is reached, the match should be declared over.

The aim of the fielding team is to prevent the batting team from scoring rounders by skilful bowling and fielding. The fielding team must have a bowler who delivers the ball to the batter and a *backstop* to stop or retrieve it. The seven remaining members of the fielding team are positioned around the pitch in the most appropriate formation for the level of play. For younger players or those just learning the game, the fielding team could be positioned with a fielder at each post and three *deep fielders* further out, beyond the running track and between the posts (*Fig 2*). With increased skill and tactical awareness the players would be moved accordingly.

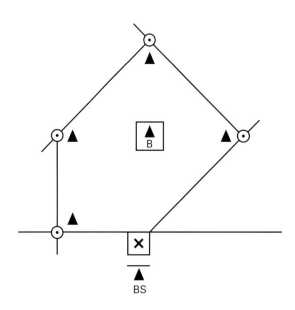

Fig 2 Basic fielding positions.

STARTING THE GAME

It is customary for the home team to toss a coin, the visiting team to call and the winner of the toss to decide whether they wish to bat or to field first. The nine batters line up on the *line for waiting batters* and wait to be called in turn to the *batting square* by the umpire. The fielding players take up their positions and, once everyone is ready, the bowler's umpire will call 'play' to start the game. The first ball is then bowled to the first batter, the *live batter*. If it is a good ball the batter must attempt a hit and then run towards first post, whether or not contact was made with the ball. The batter does not have to run on a *no ball*, but, having chosen to do so, cannot be caught out or *stumped out* at first post. If the bowler delivers two consecutive no balls to the same player, the batting team is awarded a *penalty half rounder*. As the live batter is attempting to make progress around the track, the fielding team should be trying to prevent the player from reaching either fourth post to score a rounder, or second post, to score half a rounder.

If the live batter is unable to reach fourth post before the next ball, the player may remain at any of the other posts on the way round, as long as contact with that post is made and maintained with hand or bat (*Fig 3*). The player may then progress to the next post, once the bowler has delivered the next ball to the next batter. No two batters may wait at the same post at the same time. If this occurs, the previous batter must move on to the post ahead, as directed by the umpire. Having left a post a batter may not return but must move on, even if it means that the batter ahead is stumped out. A simple way for a batter to avoid this situation is never to release a post until the one ahead is clear. A batter who hits the ball so that it pitches into the *back-ward area* may run only to first post until the ball crosses or is thrown over the *forward/backward* line. A batter who runs

Fig 3 Maintaining contact with the post.

11

past first post following such a hit will be sent back to that post by the umpire.

GETTING THE BATTER OUT

The batter is out if:

1 the ball is caught by the fielding team direct from the bat or from the hand holding the bat;
2 any part of the batter's foot projects over the front or the back line of the batting square before the ball has passed or been hit by the batter, except in the case of a no ball;
3 the batter runs to the inside of the

Fig 4 Rounders equipment.

post, unless forced to do so by a fielder causing an *obstruction*;
4 a fielder touches the post immediately ahead of the batter with the ball or the hand holding the ball, while the batter is running towards that post and before contact has been made; the exception to this is at first post in the case of a no ball;
5 the batter obstructs a fielder or intentionally deflects the course of the ball;
6 the batter overtakes another batter;
7 the batter loses contact with the post or runs at any time when the bowler is in possession of the ball in the *bowling square*, unless during an overrun behind the *2m line* or when ordered to do so by the umpire;
8 the batter has been ordered to make contact with a post and does not do so;
9 the batter drops or throws the bat deliberately.

EQUIPMENT

For safety reasons, all equipment used must be approved by the NRA (*Fig 4*).

Bat

This may be of any length up to a maximum of 46cm and should measure not more than 17cm round the thickest part. Bats may be made of wood or aluminium. If the wooden type is spliced, the joint and any binding should be tight and secure and the surface of the bat should be kept smooth and free from splinters and dirt. If the bat is made of aluminium, rubber caps and handles should be well-fitting and checked regularly. Grips and binding specifically made for rounders bats are recommended.

Ball

The ball should weigh a minimum of 65gm and a maximum of 85gm. It should measure a minimum of 18cm and a maximum of 20cm in circumference. Only NRA, white, licensed balls should be used for matches. The ball should be kept in good condition, without loose or frayed stitching, raised seams or tears. It should be free from dirt.

POSTS

Four posts are needed. Each should be 1.2m high and secured by a solid, detach-able base. The posts should not shatter, splinter or break since this may cause injury. All posts should be cylindrical in shape. Wooden posts of less than 90mm in circumference should be sheathed in plastic. Flexible posts should be avoided because of the potential whiplash effect. Lightweight alloy posts are the only metal ones permitted. Posts that are tapered to fit inside their bases should not be tapered to less than 20mm in diameter.

Bases

The circumference and weight of the base should be sufficient to ensure that the post will remain static and upright in all weather conditions. It is recommended by the NRA that the bases should be made of a rubber-like substance. Metal bases are no longer supported by the Association.

The base should have no sharp projections or points and, if there is a collar, it should be no higher than 50mm. Posts driven into the ground, without a base, are extremely dangerous and are not permitted by the rules.

Clothing and Footwear

Players should be suitably dressed in sportswear and may wear trainers, astro boots or football boots. Studs are permitted, provided that they measure more than 30mm in circumference at the base and are no longer than 12mm in length (*Fig 5*). Spikes are prohibited. All players, including the substitutes, should be clearly numbered to facilitate the calling in of the batters by the umpires and accurate recording on the score sheet.

Fig 5 Studs may be worn.

THE UMPIRES

The game is controlled by two umpires: the batter's umpire and the bowler's umpire. These are responsible for ensuring a smooth running game within the accepted rules set down by the NRA. We strongly recommend that all umpires should be affiliated to the NRA and that they participate in the NRA Award Scheme. The NRA will send an official to run local courses if there are sufficient numbers ready to participate.

Batter's Umpire

The batter's umpire stands in a position where the batter and first post may be seen without the need to turn around. A batter's umpire in the correct position should be able to see the front line of both squares and first post. Being well sighted at first post is essential, as a good fielding team will be aiming to put out the live batter at that point. It may often be a close race between the fielder and the batter, making the decision of the umpire a crucial one.

The duties of the batter's umpire are to:

1 Call 'rounder' or *'half a rounder'* and give the scores of both teams, after a rounder or half rounder has been awarded.
2 Call 'no ball' for balls that are not delivered with a smooth, underarm action.
3 Call 'no ball' for any ball bowled that passes the batter above head height or below the knee. A *donkey drop* ball must be judged carefully since it is only a no ball if it passes the batter at the incorrect height. The umpire must not prejudge such a ball, as a donkey drop will leave the bowler's hand in an upward path and may then drop into the correct height zone for the batter.
4 Call 'no ball' for a ball that hits the ground on its way to the batter.
5 Call 'no ball' if the bowler steps over the front line of the bowling square during the bowling action while still in possession of the ball. The bowler may step over this line after having released the ball.
6 Give decisions concerning the front and the back line of the batter's square, calling 'batter out' if the batter steps over the front or the back line of the square while in the process of hitting a good ball. Once the ball has been hit or missed the batter may then cross the front or the back line on the way to first post. A batter who steps over the front or the back line while attempting to hit a no ball is not out.
7 Give decisions concerning the forward/backward line. A *backward hit* is called when a ball lands behind this line; the batter concerned may then run only to first post and wait until the ball has passed into the forward area.
8 Give decisions concerning the first and the fourth post if either is stumped by a fielder. If the batter is running towards the stumped post, that batter is called 'out'. The umpire may also move players on to the next post if they have lost contact with the previous post while the ball was being played. The umpire must also call a batter 'out' if the player has lost contact with a post while the ball is in the possession of the bowler in the bowler's square.
9 Give decisions concerning all catches.
10 Call in, by name or number, the next player to bat.

11 Call 'obstruction' if the backstop steps over the 1m backstop line before the batter has attempted a hit.

Bowler's Umpire

The bowler's umpire should initially stand behind second post or between the second and the third post, making sure that the view of both the bowler and the batter is unobstructed (*Fig 6*).

The duties of the bowler's umpire are to:

1   Call 'play' at the beginning of each innings and to restart the game after a *dead-ball* situation .
2   Call 'no ball' for *wides* if the ball passes beyond the normal reach of the batter. This includes bowling to the wrong side of the batter. The umpire must judge a no ball on the position of the batter as the ball is being bowled and not as the batter moves to hit it. It is the batter's fault if he or she moves into or draws away from the ball.
3   Call 'no ball' for any ball that hits or would have hit the batter had the player remained in his or her original position.
4   Call 'no ball' if the bowler's foot projects over the back or side lines of the bowling square.
5   Give decisions concerning the second and the third post regarding stumpings, obstruction, early release by the batter and running inside the track.
6   Ensure that the waiting batters and those who are out are behind their respective lines. If they are not behind the lines and they obstruct the fielders a penalty half rounder shall be awarded to the fielding team.
7   Call 'half a rounder' if the live batter, having hit the ball, reaches second post and nullify that half rounder if the batter is out off the same ball before reaching fourth post.

Both Umpires

The duties of both umpires are to:

1   Check the playing area and make sure that the pitch is clear of obstructions.
2   Check all equipment, clothing and

Fig 6 Umpires' starting position.

footwear in accordance with the NRA safety policy.

3   Keep score sheets and control the game.
4   Keep a check on players who are out.
5   Work as a team and consult each other over decisions where there is any doubt.
6   Change positions at the completion of two batting innings.
7   Call all decisions loudly and clearly so that all players and the other umpire may hear.
8   Warn and, if necessary, send off any player who has committed an unsporting act. This also applies to a bowler who is bowling in a dangerous manner.

Either umpire who sees an incident which is not relevant to his or her specific duties should bring it to the attention of the other. The final decision rests with the umpire whose duty it concerns. A typical example of this would be when a batter leaves first post while the bowler is still in the process of bowling. The batter's umpire may miss this while concentrating on the next batter receiving a ball. The bowler's umpire should bring this to the attention of the other umpire, who must then decide whether to call that batter 'out'.

A controversial event may occur requiring consultation between the umpires. In this situation the unsighted or doubtful umpire should ask for a second opinion. This should be done quietly and the outcome should be announced in the usual way. If the umpires fail to agree, the final decision rests with the umpire who is responsible for that area of the game. Depending on the age and skill level of the players, the umpires may decide to waive certain rules, but this must remain within the safety recommendations and be agreeable to both teams. It is always a good idea to discuss the following:

1   the number of innings, normally two each;
2   duration of an innings or the number of good balls;
3   which rules are to be waived;
4   each umpire's responsibilities.

The umpires should move, when appropriate, to ensure a clear view of all incidents concerning their posts. The batter's umpire should stay in position until the live batter has reached first post, then move across towards fourth post as the live batter proceeds around the track. Thus the batter's umpire has a clear view of the live batter approaching fourth post and is in an excellent position to judge whether a rounder has been scored or whether the batter is out. The bowler's umpire moves between the second and the fourth post, keeping well clear of the players. Both umpires require a certain degree of all-round fitness, good eyesight and peripheral vision. A static umpire is a bad one (*Fig 7*).

SCORING

One Rounder

a   One rounder may be scored from any one hit. In the case of a no ball which is hit and caught, the batter may still score in the usual way.
b   One rounder shall be scored if, after hitting the ball, the batter succeeds in running round the track, touching

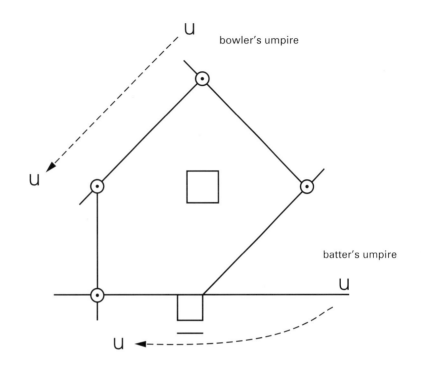

Fig 7 Movement of the umpires during the game

bowler's umpire

batter's umpire

fourth post or runs on from first post when the ball has been returned to the forward area after a backward hit, provided that :
i)   the live batter has not overtaken any other batter;
ii) the bowler has not delivered another ball;
iii) while the live batter was waiting at a post, the post ahead was not touched by a fielder with the ball.

Half a Rounder

a   Half a rounder shall be scored if the live batter completes the track, fulfilling the same conditions as for scoring one rounder but without hitting the ball.
b   Half a rounder shall be scored if the live batter, having hit the ball, reaches

second post, but should the batter continue their run and be put out off the same ball before reaching fourth post, the score will be nullified.

Penalty Half Rounder

A penalty half rounder shall be awarded if:

a   the bowler delivers two consecutive no balls to the same batter; after a penalty half rounder has been awarded for two consecutive no balls, the previous no balls are cancelled and the count starts again;
b   a fielder obstructs a batter (*Fig 8*) (this also applies if the backstop steps over the *backstop line* before the batter has attempted a hit;
c   a waiting batter or batter out obstructs a fielder.

Fig 8 A penalty half rounder is awarded for obstruction by a fielder.

Carlton v Lenford

DATE 25th May 1999

FIRST INNINGS				SECOND INNINGS			
Good Balls	**Batter**	**Balls Order**	**Rounders**	**Batter**	**Balls Order**	**Good Balls**	**Rounders**
1 11 21	V. Hughes	• •		V. Hughes	• • • •	1 11 21	½ 1 1 1
2 12 22	J. Davies	• • • •	1½ ½ 1	J. Davies	• • •	2 12 22	1 ½
3 13 23	A. Jameson	• • •	1 1	A. Jameson	• • •	3 13 23	½2
4 14 24	R. Patel	:• • •	1	R. Patel	• • •	4 14 24	1½
5 15 25	R. Head	• • •	½	R. Head	•	5 15 25	
6 16 26	J. Thomas	• •	½	J. Thomas	• ••	6 16 26	
7 17 27	S. Short	• • •	½ 1½	S. Short	• • •	7 17 27	1
8 18 28	A. Boynton	• •	½	S. Jones	• • •	8 18 28	½ ½½
9 19 29	D. Hilditch	• • •	1 1	D. Hilditch	• • •	9 19 29	½ 1
10 20 30	Reserves S. Jones			Reserves A. Boynton		10 20 30	
obstruction: ½				obstruction: ½			
2 consecutive no balls: ½				2 consecutive no balls:			
		TOTAL	12½			FINAL TOTAL	24

Fig 9 Sample score sheet.

One Rounder and One Penalty Half Rounder

It should be noted that a rounder may be scored with the addition of the award of:

a one penalty half rounder, if the ball that is hit is the second consecutive no ball to that batter;

b one penalty half rounder if the batter is obstructed;

c two penalty half rounders if both (a) and (b) apply.

Score Sheet

A comprehensive score sheet may appear daunting at first (*Fig 9*), but once mastered it facilitates the smooth and efficient running of the game. All players may be called in by name and each ball can be recorded as it is bowled. No balls, obstructions and methods by which players are dismissed are recorded, thus providing an accurate and useful record of events.

The umpire should wait for a dead ball situation to fill in the score sheet, otherwise an important incident may be missed. Batters should not enter the batting square until called in by the batter's umpire, thereby allowing time for the umpires to record relevant information. Both umpires should complete a score sheet to avoid any errors or discrepancies (*Fig 10*).

CAPTAIN'S DUTIES

The captain should take responsibility for the team and at all times lead by example.

1 The home captain tosses the coin and invites the visiting captain to call 'heads' or 'tails'; the winning captain then decides whether to bat or field first and notifies the umpire accordingly.

2 The captain gives the batting order to the umpires before each innings; any substitutions should be notified during the course of the innings.

3 The captain should set the field according to the strengths and weaknesses of both teams.

4 The captain should be ready to change the bowler whenever necessary.

Fig 10 National Rounders Association umpire.

19

5　When appropriate, the captain should assist the fielders by indicating which one should attempt to catch or retrieve the ball; uncalled catches can cause confusion and may lead to injury.

6　Safety checks are made by the umpires but the captains should check that their teams have the appropriate clothing and footwear; numbered bibs or shirts should be organized if necessary.

7　At all times the captains should display sportsmanship and leadership.

8　At the end of the match the captains should congratulate the opposition and thank the umpires.

2

Basic Skills

The basic skills of rounders are running, batting, bowling and fielding. In order to excel at these a rounders player requires speed, accuracy, strength and co-ordination. Good basic skills should be taught to beginners, but individual styles will emerge as players gain experience. It would be wrong to be dogmatic about batting stance or catching techniques with a young player who consistently hits great rounders and never drops a ball, but players who practise the correct skills from the start frequently achieve greater success.

Regular, structured practice is invaluable for the developing player. Competitive sessions and matches will increase tactical awareness, but the individual requires a balanced programme of coaching and competition.

RUNNING

Running is often neglected as a specific skill. It should be coached and practised along with batting, fielding and bowling. Running skill can be improved with better fitness and attention to technique, particularly that involved in cornering.

Running Around the Track

The batter should accelerate out of the batting square with a high leg sprinting action, a lowered centre of gravity, long strides and pumping arms. As first post is approached, speed should be reduced and the left shoulder dropped as the body leans towards the post. Maximum speed should be attained on the straight parts of the track. This is particularly so on the final straight to fourth post. Should the batter need to stop at a post, the 2m line allows for braking distance, but the post should be touched before the overrun (*Fig 11*).

Fig 11 Running is an important skill.

Batting

This is one of the most difficult skills to perfect. The shape of the bat, the small size of the ball and the varied speed and height of the bowler's delivery make the skill of striking the ball a tricky one. This is particularly so for young players who will need a great deal of practice and guidance to ensure a sound technique.

The aim of the batter is to score rounders. This may be done by hitting the ball as hard and as far as possible. More importantly, however, a batter should be accurate in placing the ball and able to vary the distance and height according to the position of the fielders.

Grip

See *Fig 12*.
1 A 'V' is formed between the thumb and the first finger of the batting hand.
2 The handle is gripped as if shaking hands with the bat.

Fig 13 Shoulder extended backwards.

Fig 12 Grip on the bat.

Fig 14 Bat held more centrally.

Fig 15 A good batting stance.

3   The bat is held firmly, with a relaxed shoulder and forearm.
4   The wrist is kept firm and cocked slightly backwards.

Stance

1   The batter stands sideways in the batter's square with the non-batting shoulder pointing in the direction that the ball should travel.
2   The batting shoulder is extended backwards in the ready position (*Fig 13*). Alternatively, the bat may be held by both hands in a more central position (*Fig 14).*

3   Feet are in line with the shoulders and comfortably apart.
4   The weight is on the back foot and the knees are slightly flexed (*Fig 15).*
5   Eyes are firmly fixed on the ball until contact is made.

Swing

1   As the ball is not always delivered in an ideal position, the swing should be adapted accordingly.
2   The bat is taken back as the ball approaches, to a position in line with the height and flight of the ball.
3   The batting arm is bent at the elbow to

23

Fig 16 Bat is held parallel to the ground during the swing.

Fig 17 Follow through with the bat.

approximately a right angle, but should straighten on contact with the ball.

4 The swing should take a continuous path around the axis of the shoulder.

5 The non-batting arm may be raised to aid balance.

6 The bat is parallel to the ground and the wrist is flexed as contact is made with the ball. This is the critical moment in batting (*Fig 16*).

7 After contact is made, the bat should follow through in the desired direction of the ball (*Fig 17*).

Fig 18 Backhand hit.

Fig 19 A flick of the wrist and fingers can add spin to the ball.

Timing of the Hit

1 The weight is transferred from the back to the front foot.
2 The weight of the upper body is transferred through the batting swing.
3 The flight of the ball should be carefully watched and the moment of contact anticipated.

Backhand Hit

See *Fig 18*. Once a consistently proficient batting action has been achieved, the batter may wish to acquire this difficult skill. The batter takes up a normal stance within the square with both hands on the bat. As the ball is bowled the upper body is rotated, bringing the bat into the backhand position. This permits a strike to the right-hand side, which inevitably takes the fielding team by surprise. A gap may usually be found between the forward/backward line and first post.

BOWLING

The main aim of the bowler is to deliver the ball to the backstop, thus preventing the batter from making contact. The bowler may also try to tempt the batter into hitting a high, catchable ball. This can be done by varying the speed and the height of the ball and the angle of delivery.

Speed

This may be increased by using the full depth of the bowler's box to maximize the transfer of weight from the back to the front foot. Rotation and transfer of weight through the upper body adds impetus to the arm swing. A final flick of the wrist

Figs 20 and 21 The bowler's smooth continuous action.

Fig 22 Bowler's grip.

and fingers can add spin to the ball (*Fig 19*).

Height

Within the permitted bowling limits a variety of balls may be delivered. A low delivery may lead to a lifted ball off the bat, resulting in a catch. A higher ball may prevent an effective swing by the batter.

Angle of Delivery

The position of the bowler within the bowling square will affect the angle of delivery. A ball that crosses the batter's square diagonally is the most difficult one to hit.

Grip

See *Fig 22*. The ball should be held in the fingers supported by the thumb. If it is held in the palm of the hand a delayed release may result in a no ball.

Swing

See *Figs 20 and 21*. The bowler's swing must be a smooth and continuous, underarm action resulting in the release of the ball. A dummy bowl is not permitted. To achieve more speed, the ball should be released at the lowest point of the swing. To induce a catch, the ball should be released during the upward swing of the arm.

Fig 23 Hands cupped to receive the ball.

Fig 24 Giving in to the body as the ball is caught.

Figs 26–30 Retrieving and throwing the ball.

Fig 26

Fig 25 A right-handed gate.

Fig 27

Fig 28

Fig 29

Fig 30

FIELDING

The role of the fielder is to prevent the batting team from scoring. A good fielder should be able to catch, stop or retrieve the ball efficiently. A quick decision followed by an accurate throw is essential. All fielders should also be prepared to cover posts, back up throws and communicate with their team mates.

Catching

See *Figs 23 and 24*. The flight of the ball should be anticipated and the fielder should move into position for a two-handed catch where possible. The arms should be bent with the elbows close in to the body. Thumbs are together, fingers are relaxed and spread to cup the ball. Keeping the arms flexed, the cupped hands move to meet and take the ball, giving in towards the body to absorb the pace. The eyes should follow the ball safely into the hands. A ball that is hit or thrown powerfully will require more give as it is caught.

Stopping

See *Fig 25*. The direction and the speed of the ball should be assessed and the fielder should try to move into the correct position behind the ball. The *gate position* should be adopted to make an effective barrier.

Given enough time, a right-handed fielder should adopt a right-facing gate since this allows the throwing action to begin while the ball is still on the ground. This is the *dynamic throwing position.*

Retrieving

See *Figs 26 to 30*. If the fielder fails to make a catch or stop the ball, it will have

Fig 31 A left-handed player retrieving the ball.

to be retrieved. This may be a difficult task since there will be several variables to cope with, such as the nature of the playing surface and the spin and the speed of the ball. A right-handed fielder must position the right foot to the left of the ball. As the ball is picked up, the body is rotated to face the direction of the throw. The opposite applies to the left-handed fielder (*Fig 31*).

Decision Making

Having fielded the ball, the fielder must decide quickly on the next course of action. The options would include:

a throwing to a fielder at a post to stump out the live batter or prevent a rounder or half a rounder;

b throwing to a fielder at a post to either

Fig 32 Cover at third post.

Fig 33 Cover at fourth post.

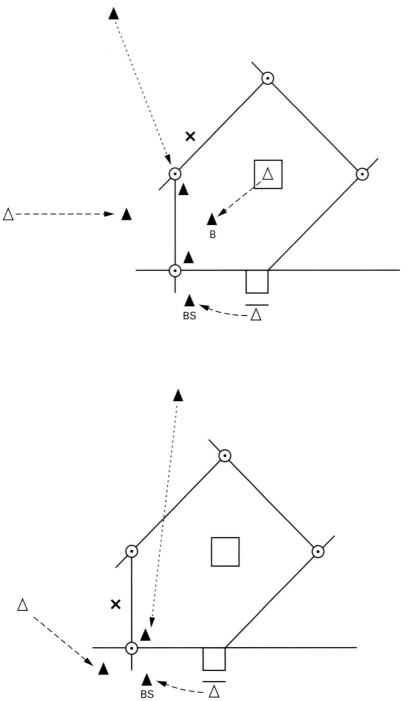

Fig 34 Suggested movement of players for covering third post.

Fig 35 Suggested movement of players for covering fourth post.

stump out or prevent the further progress of a previous batter;

c   throwing to the bowler to prevent any further movement around the posts;

d   throwing to the backstop to stump the batting square to end an innings.

Overarm Throwing

The ball is taken behind the throwing shoulder with a flexed arm. Rotation of the upper body and the follow-through of the arm in the direction of the throw ensure strength and accuracy. The body weight is transferred from the back to the front foot during the throwing action. Finally, the throwing arm is straightened and the back foot follows through.

Covering

See *Figs 32 to 35*. A triangle of cover should be set up around the appropriate post to await the return of the ball. The cover depends primarily on the direction of the hit and fielders must be prepared to be flexible when covering. The receiver must be within stumping distance of the post, supported by at least one other fielder in case there is an overthrow or misfield. A third fielder would be useful in the event of a wide throw. The fielders should anticipate the flight of the ball and reposition themselves accordingly. Deep fielders should walk in as the ball is being bowled, in readiness for action.

Communication

The bowler and the backstop should use signals to indicate the type of ball being bowled. The backstop is in the best position to assess the likely strike and set the field accordingly. Once the ball has been struck, the appropriate fielder should call to indicate an intention of fielding the ball, thus avoiding any confusion. Good communication often results in more than one batter being out on a single ball. The covering fielders should make their presence known, so that the post fielders may confidently remain within stumping distance of their posts.

3
Advanced Skills and Positional Play

PLAYING A POSITION

A young player should have the experience of playing in all positions before making a particular choice.

The rotation of players from an early age ensures the development of every skill. Players with versatility are more likely to be selected at international level, although occasionally a prolific scorer may not be a good fielder. Within the present rules, only nine out of fifteen squad members are on the pitch at one time, so some players may only be utilized in one position. *Fig 36* shows the qualities required by a rounders player. Some will excel in certain areas, making them more obvious candidates for specific positions.

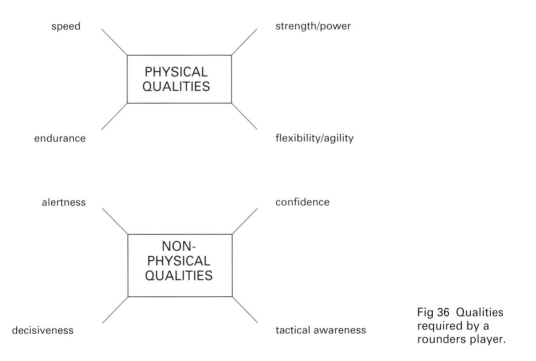

Fig 36 Qualities required by a rounders player.

BOWLER

The bowler must deliver a consistently good ball . This should be difficult to hit and the bowler should influence the batter's strike with a variety of balls. The bowler's repertoire should include the following:

1 fast delivery to the backstop;
2 ball bowled as close to the body as possible;
3 angled delivery;
4 donkey drop;
5 spin delivery.

Fast Delivery

See *Fig 37*. This type of ball should be difficult to hit and it is tactically useful against a weaker batter. A skilful batter, however, is likely to convert the speed of delivery into a powerful hit.

TECHNIQUE

Maximize the space available in the bowling square. This may be done in several ways:

a   Stand at the back of the square with the left side facing the batter. Step sideways with the left foot, bringing the right arm behind and close the right foot up to the left. Now step forward with the left foot, bend that knee, rotate the shoulders and swing through with the right arm to deliver the ball at the lowest point of the swing (*Fig 38*).

Fig 37 A fast delivery is difficult to hit.

Fig 38 A low release for a fast delivery.

b Face second post, turn and run round the back of the square. Transfer the weight from the back to the front foot as the arm swings through to deliver the ball.

c Stand at the back of the square and hold the ball with the bowling arm across the body. Step on to the right foot as the bowling arm swings back across the body to the underarm bowling position. The arm continues the bowling action and the weight is transferred on to the left foot. Once the ball has been released, momentum should carry the body forward out of the bowling square.

Ball Bowled Close to the Body

See *Fig 39*. This type of ball, if delivered within the rules, is one of the most difficult to hit as the batter must adjust the body position in order to make contact with the ball. If the ball is bowled at speed it becomes almost impossible to hit since the batter has so little time in which to react. Reduced visibility may cause problems for the backstop, however and a trade-off between speed and accuracy may be required.

TECHNIQUE

As for fast bowling, but aiming to just miss the batter's body. This type of ball requires much practice to perfect and umpires may be quick to call a body ball as they see the batter move aside. Initially, a reduced backswing and a shorter run up may help to improve accuracy.

Angled Delivery

See *Figs 40 to 42*. This type of ball is deceptive as it approaches at an angle rather than head-on. A right-handed

Fig 39 Bowl as close to the body as possible.

Fig 40 Varied
angles of delivery.

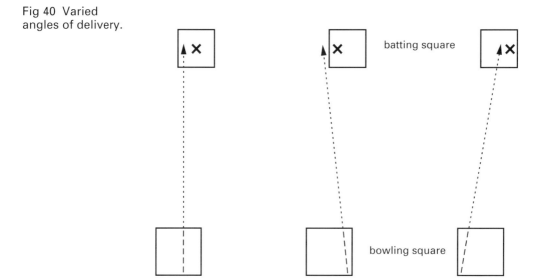

batting square

bowling square

Fig 41 A deceptively angled ball.

Fig 42 A left-handed bowler may produce a more angled delivery.

batter will have great difficulty in coping with a ball that travels from right to left.

TECHNIQUE

As for fast bowling, but the positioning within the bowling square is important. Stand close to the side at the back of the square in order to maximize the angle to the batter, delivering the ball from the front corner.

Donkey Drop

See *Figs 43 to 45.* This is a high and slow ball which drops to the correct height as it reaches the batter. It may also be a frustrating ball as the batter may have difficulty in judging its speed of descent. It is tactically useful against a strong batter since it interrupts the normal batting action, causing an upward hit and leading to a possible catch.

TECHNIQUE

Stand with feet apart in the middle of the square, since this ball requires less

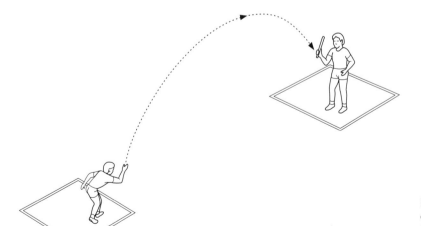

Fig 43 The donkey drop ball falls to the correct height at the last moment.

39

Figs 44 and 45 The donkey drop.

momentum. Transfer the weight to the left foot as the arm swings through and release the ball on the upward motion, allowing it to rise steeply. This requires less back swing than the fast ball. Aim for a high point approximately three-quarters of the distance between the front line of the bowling square and the batter. This ball also requires a great deal of practice as there is a high risk of its being a no ball.

Spin Bowling

See *Fig 46*. This type of ball is both deceptive and unnerving and a good spin bowler may be a real asset to a team. If contact is made it may sometimes be off the edge of the bat, travelling backwards and giving a catch to the backstop.

TECHNIQUE
As for fast bowling, but at the moment of release the wrist and fingers are sharply flicked either outwards or inwards, depending on the desired spin. An outward flick of the wrist and fingers will produce a ball which appears to be going wide until the last moment. The underarm follow-through should be across the body. An inward flick of the wrist and fingers will produce a ball which appears to be too close to the body.

Fig 46 Spin bowling is a useful technique.

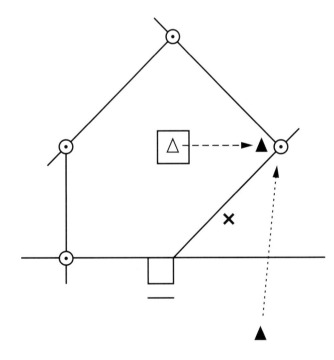

Fig 47 Bowler moves to cover first post.

Fig 48 Bowler
moves to cover
third post.

The underarm follow-through should be slightly wide of the body.

Covering

The bowler's role is not over when the ball has been delivered. The next requirement is to catch, field or cover.

The bowler may be required to cover at any of the posts. First-post cover may be appropriate if the post fielder is playing deep (*Fig 47*). In the absence of the second- or the third-post fielder the bowler should assume those post positions when the ball is being returned from the deep field. If the post fielders are present then they should provide cover for them (*Fig 48*). Fourth-post cover would be appropriate only in certain circumstances. If the ball has been hit just in front of the forward/backward line and the fourth-post fielder has had to move away from the post because the third deep fielder was slow to react, then the bowler should cover.

The bowler is therefore a key member of the fielding team. Communication with the backstop and the first-post fielder is vital as they must know what ball to expect. Even an international bowler has the occasional 'off day' and should have the strength of character to accept substitution since games may be lost on no balls. In addition to these skills, the bowler must remain calm under pressure in order to enable the correct decisions to be made throughout the game. A good bowler should be complemented by an equally good backstop and the two should train together to develop a close rapport.

BACKSTOP

The backstop should be an agile, dynamic player with quick reactions. The role of the backstop is to catch or stop the ball as efficiently as possible from the bowler's delivery, sending it to the appropriate

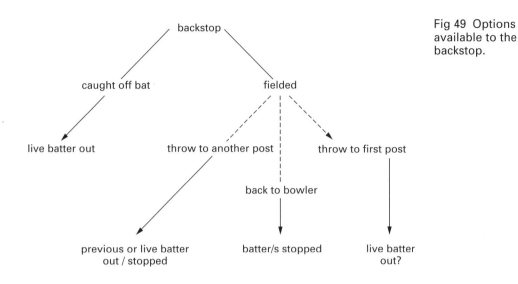

Fig 49 Options available to the backstop.

fielder. There are several options available (see *Fig 49*):

Positioning

The backstop should align with the bowler in accordance with the batter's position and the expected delivery. It is important to stand behind the bat, not the batter, in order to keep a clear view of the bowler and the incoming ball, but care must be taken not to step over the backstop line before the batter has attempted a hit. The weight should be evenly distributed with the legs flexed. The feet should be comfortably apart, either parallel or astride, providing a stable base from which to receive the ball on either side. As the ball is taken, the correct throwing position is adopted. To receive the ball, the hands should be held up in front of the body to act as a target for the bowler and the thumbs should be together with the palms spread to create a barrier. The ball should be caught before it bounces (*Figs 50 and 51*).

Fig 50 Backstop with feet parallel.

Fig 51 Backstop with feet astride.

Fig 52 Backstop may choose to throw to fourth post.

Protective clothing, including helmet, gloves and pads may be worn.

Decision Making

Using any prior knowledge of the batter, the backstop can assist the bowler in deciding on the most appropriate delivery. This partnership is essential to a successful fielding team. Before each ball is bowled, the backstop should be aware of the position of the batters on the track and also of the fielders. Throwing to first post may not always be the best course of action if a stronger batter can be stumped out at another post, particularly the fourth. A quick thinking backstop may

be instrumental in the dismissal of more than one player on the same ball (*Fig 52*).

Throwing

The backstop's throw should be extremely accurate and to the inside of the post in order to avoid hitting the batter or causing the receiver to obstruct (*Fig 53*). In the event of a backward hit the backstop should attempt to catch the player out. If this is not possible, the batter will be prevented from running past first post if the backstop delays the return of the ball over the forward/backward line. Another option would be to throw straight to second post,

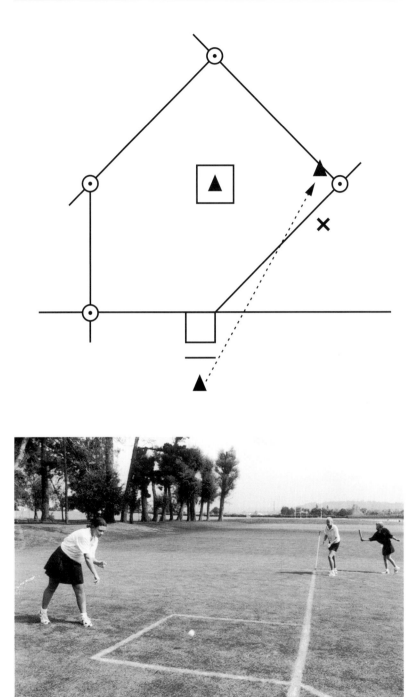

Fig 53 Backstop must throw the ball to the inside of the post to avoid the possibility of obstruction.

Fig 54 Putting the side out.

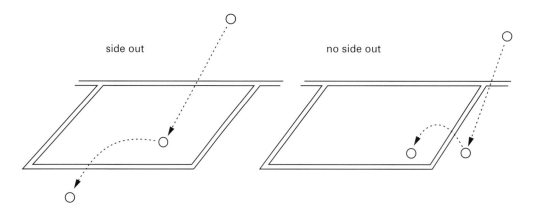

Fig 55 Side out; the ball has pitched direct into the batting square.

Fig 56 No side out; the ball has pitched outside and then rolled into the batting square.

Fig 57 First-post fielder is too close to the post.

anticipating the batter's continued run as the ball crosses that line. Alternatively, the backstop may wish to throw to another post in order to stump out a previous batter.

Covering

There may not be a fourth-post fielder, so the backstop must take responsibility for this post, usually covered by the first-post fielder. In any event, the backstop must be prepared to move quickly towards fourth post at any time in the game.

Stumping the Box

If there are no waiting batters, the backstop or any other fielder should attempt to pitch or place the ball into the batting square before the leading batter touches fourth post. This will put the whole *side out (Fig 54)*. A ball which rolls or bounces into the batting square will not put the side out *(Figs 55 and 56)*.

Fig 58 First post fielder is in the correct position.

Fig 59 The essential fielding triangle.

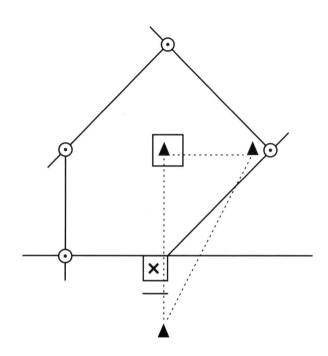

Fig 60 The positions of bowler, backstop and first-post fielder

FIRST-POST FIELDER

The ability to catch a hard and fast throw is paramount, as the first-post fielder's primary role is to receive the ball from the backstop and stump out the live batter. This must be achieved without causing an obstruction on the running track since this will result in the batter's remaining in and being awarded a penalty half rounder.

Positioning

The first-post fielder should stand inside the post, at an arm's distance from it, thereby attracting the throw from the backstop or the bowler to the inside of the track (*Figs 57 and 58*). A left-handed player may be useful here as the left hand

is nearer to the post, enabling a quicker stumping. Catching and stumping should be practised without actually looking at the post. The first-post fielder is the third member of the essential fielding triangle, comprising the bowler, the backstop and first post (*Figs 59 and 60*).

Decision Making

In receiving the ball from backstop or bowler, the first-post fielder should attempt to stump out the batter running to first post. Whether successful or not, a throw to another post, particularly the second or fourth, must be considered since it is possible to stump out more than one player on one ball. It may, however, be more appropriate to return the ball to the bowler. A good tactical

Fig 61 Stumping out at first post; note the deep field covering.

understanding and awareness of the game situation is essential (*Fig 61*).

Covering

The first-post fielder should back up the bowler when the ball is returned from the deep field beyond the third and the fourth post. If the back stop moves to take fourth post then the first-post fielder should replace the backstop as fourth-post cover (*Fig 62*).

First Post Playing as a Deep Fielder

When a left-handed player is batting, the first-post player must be prepared to move to the deep field. It may be necessary to retrieve a ball hit deep into the backward area on that side. In certain circumstances the field may be set without a first-post fielder, moving that player into the deep field beyond first post. Usually this would be whenever there is only one remaining batter or when the opposition have strong hitters.

SECOND-POST FIELDER

The second-post fielder usually plays off the post as an extra deep fielder. The bowler's action may obstruct that fielder's view of the bat so quick reactions are necessary. Having fielded the ball, the second-post fielder has several options. If the live batter is running towards second post and there is the possibility of stumping that post

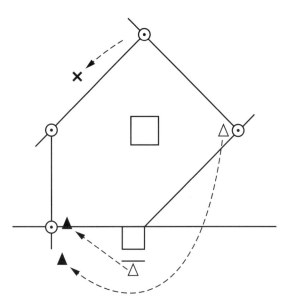

Fig 62 First-post fielder replaces backstop as fourth-post cover.

without causing an obstruction, this should be attempted, as this will prevent a half rounder. In the same situation, if the bowler has taken up a position at second post, it would be more appropriate to throw to that post, avoiding obstruction completely. If the batter has passed second post, a throw to the bowler in the bowling square could be the best option or, if it seems likely that a rounder may be scored, a throw to third or fourth post could prevent this. The second-post fielder covers all throws from the backstop to the bowler.

THIRD-POST FIELDER

A great number of balls hit by right-handed batters will travel in the direction of third post. This may not be the case at an international level, but it certainly applies with less experienced players. The third-post fielder, therefore, should be an excellent catcher with quick reactions, and the confidence to attempt to take even the most difficult catches. If the opposition's hitters are relatively weak the third-post fielder may stand inside the post, ready to move forward when necessary to take a short catch. Fielding options include stumping third post, a throw to the bowler covering third post or a throw to the fourth post, depending on the batter's position. If the batter has stopped at first or second post, a return to the bowler will prevent further movement around the track. The third-post player should cover all throws from first post to the bowler.

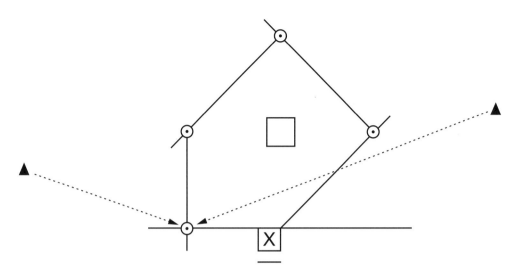

Fig 63 The first deep fielder has the longest throw to fourth post though the fielders are the same distance from the batter.

FOURTH-POST FIELDER

This fielder is always under pressure because any mistakes usually result in a rounder being conceded. Excellent catching skills, quick reactions, good peripheral vision and the ability to remain calm are all essential requirements of this position. Correct positioning inside the post, within an arm's reach of it, is vital as there is no time for repositioning once the ball has been caught. There is nothing more frustrating for a fielder than to throw to fourth post only to find that the player is too far away from it to make a quick stumping. This happens frequently at school level, as the fourth-post fielder is inclined to move towards the deep fielder to shorten the return throw. The rounder is conceded and, worse still, a penalty half rounder may be awarded for obstruction!

If a strong batter is waiting at third post

and the live batter misses the ball, the fourth-post fielder must anticipate a quick throw from the backstop. It might then be possible to get another batter out on the running track. Against a strong batting team the fourth-post fielder may be utilized as an extra deep fielder and fourth post would be covered by the backstop.

DEEP FIELDERS

These players should be alert, quick off the mark and agile, with good catching and retrieving skills. Contrary to popular belief, this is not a static position! Repositioning is necessary with every batter and with every ball bowled. Walking in from a deep position will facilitate anticipation of the strike and prepare the body to move in any direction. The deep fielder should try to stop the ball as

51

quickly and as efficiently as possible, being confident enough to attempt a catch, knowing that if the ball is missed there will be cover in place behind. Calling for a catch and indicating where cover is present will assist the other fielders.

As a general guide, if the live batter has reached second post before the deep fielder has collected the ball, it is essential to throw direct to fourth post to prevent a rounder. The fielder with the strongest and most accurate throw should be placed as first deep fielder if the opposition are hitting in that direction, since the distance of the return throw to fourth post is the longest (*Fig 63*). The first deep fielder should also cover the throw from the backstop to first post. The second deep fielder should cover the second and the third post in the event of a throw from inside the track, and the third deep fielder should cover a throw to fourth post from the first deep fielder. The deep fielders should always cover each other.

4
Skills Practices

Practices need to be tailored to the needs of the individual or the team in order to make them most effective. If performance steadily improves, then practices are obviously suitable. If performance is not improving then practices must be unsuitable. The old saying that 'practice makes perfect' is not strictly true. Inappropriate practice will demoralize players instead of inspiring them and in many cases it may be worse than no practice at all.

Feedback is an essential component of training and without it little or no learning will result. Video cameras are useful to record matches and they should be used throughout training programmes, particularly in the early stages of skills development.

Complex skills may need to be broken down into stages and practised separately. The first-post fielder should be able to catch the ball and stump the post in one action; but catching and stumping may be practised as different skills then combined as a single movement.

Frequency, duration, intensity and types of practice are of equal importance and they are all variables in coaching. Quality is more important than quantity since repeating a skill badly only reinforces the incorrect movement pattern, making correction yet more difficult. Practices should also be realistic. If a backstop practices each time with a bowler but no batter that is obviously unrealistic. It would be perfectly acceptable as an initial practice, provided that a batter is added at a later stage.

In skills such as batting there should be a balance between speed and accuracy. In some certain circumstances a slower, accurate hit away from fielders would be more appropriate than a powerful, carelessly placed drive. Finally, safety is of paramount importance. Young children should start with soft balls and the careful spacing of players during practices should prevent accidents with the bat or ball. If players do not have studs a slippery pitch may be dangerous, so plan a more static practice for wet days.

RUNNING PRACTICES

Running as a skill is often overlooked because it may appear as an obvious requirement. Good running technique may make a half chance into a rounder, particularly when a fielding error occurs. All players need to be coached in sprinting and effective cornering while maintaining awareness of the game going on around them. Players should carry a bat to make the practices more realistic (*Fig 64*).

Fig 64.

Individual Practices

1 Jog around the rounders pitch.
2 Sprint to first post from the batting square, jog around second post to third post and sprint to fourth post (*Fig 65*).
3 As above, but sprint all the way around the track. Timing would introduce a competitive element to this activity and should increase motivation.

Fig 65.

Pairs Practices

1 The first runner sprints from the batting square towards first post. As the player reaches the post his or her partner sets off from the same place and attempts to catch up before the first runner touches fourth post.
2 Each player sets off at the same time and tries to be first back to the starting cone, running anticlockwise and carrying a bat. The emphasis is on speed around the cones and tight cornering (*Fig 66*).
3 Relay shuttle, competing against other pairs and passing a bat. Running anticlockwise keeps the practice realistic (*Fig 67*).

Group Practices

BEAT THE BALL
Groups of four; one player runs anticlockwise around three cones 12m apart, trying to beat the ball that is being thrown around the cones by the three other players. The ball must be thrown around

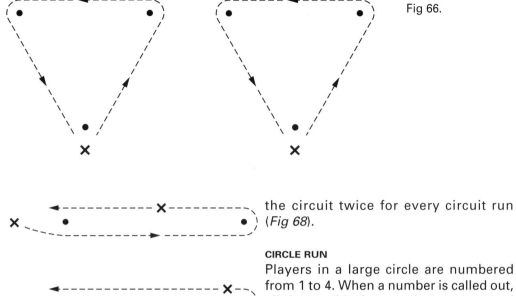

Fig 66.

Fig 67 Relay shuttle with bats.

the circuit twice for every circuit run (*Fig 68*).

CIRCLE RUN
Players in a large circle are numbered from 1 to 4. When a number is called out, all those with that number race around the circle in an anticlockwise direction, attempting to be the first one back (*Fig 69*).

Fig 68 Beat the ball.

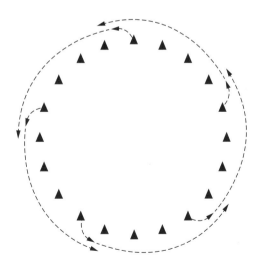

Fig 69 Circle run.

Fig 70 Pass and
go.

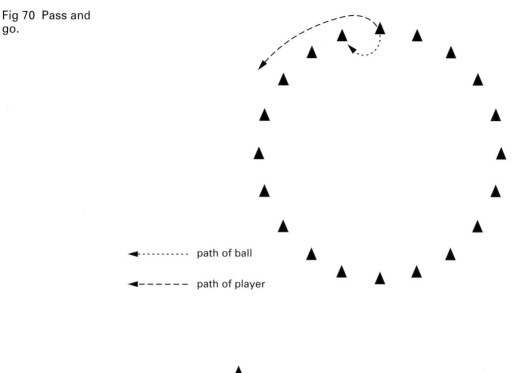

········ path of ball

－－－－ path of player

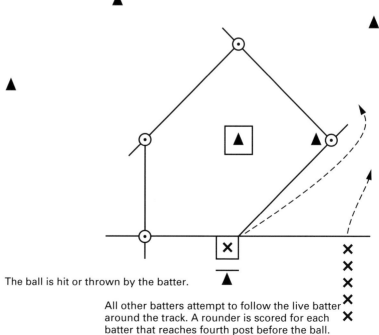

The ball is hit or thrown by the batter.

Fig 71 Team beat
the ball.

All other batters attempt to follow the live batter
around the track. A rounder is scored for each
batter that reaches fourth post before the ball.

PASS AND GO

One player passes a ball underarm to the next player on the right then runs anti-clockwise around the circle back to his or her place. As soon as the player receiving the ball has passed it on, he or she follows the previous runner. Players should not overtake those in front of them. Younger children enjoy this practice as they usually just get back to their place in time to receive the ball again (*Fig 70*).

TEAM BEAT THE BALL

Two teams of six; the first batter throws the ball out as far as possible and sets off for first post. The rest of the team are lined up behind the forward/backward line opposite first post. They follow the batter all the way round the track as far as possible. The ball is returned by the fielding team to first post then thrown around the posts in turn, trying to beat the runners. A rounder is scored for every player reaching fourth post before the ball. This practice may be done with the batter striking or throwing the ball, depending upon the skill levels (*Fig 71*).

AEROBIC ROUNDERS

The waiting batters line up behind the backstop. They must all run to a point in between two posts and return on every

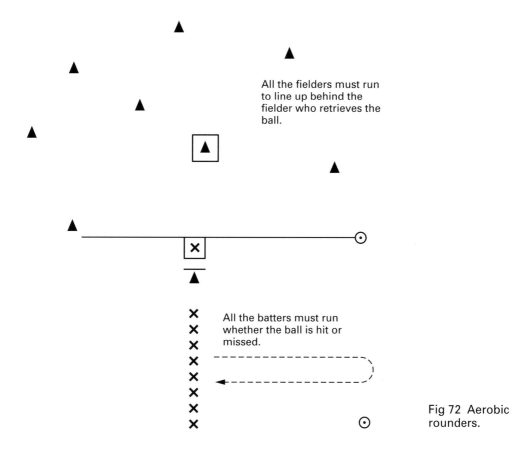

All the fielders must run to line up behind the fielder who retrieves the ball.

All the batters must run whether the ball is hit or missed.

Fig 72 Aerobic rounders.

ball. The fielding team must line up behind the fielder who collects the ball. If the batting team are first, they score a rounder. If the fielding team are first, the batters are out. Every player gets a good aerobic work-out in this game which is particularly suitable for younger players (*Fig 72*).

THROWING AND CATCHING PRACTICES

Beanbags, small, soft balls, tennis balls or rounders balls may be used for most of these practices. A softer version of a rounders ball, the *Incrediball* is ideal for younger players.

Individual Practices

1   Standing, throw the ball underarm up to a height of 2m and catch it using both hands. Progress to catching with either hand.
2   Standing, throw the ball progressively higher and catch it using both hands. Progress to one hand (*Fig 73*).
3   Walking slowly, throw the ball up to a comfortable height and catch it using both hands. Progress to one hand.
4   As before, throw the ball progressively higher, increasing the speed and moving to a position under the ball.
5   Throw the ball up into the air and see how many times the player may clap,

Fig 73 Static one-handed catch.

Fig 74 Practice for younger children.

58

Fig 75 Different ways of throwing.

sit down or shout a word, spin or touch the ground before catching the ball with both hands and then with one hand; younger players enjoy this exercise (*Fig 74*).

6 Throw the ball into the air in as many different ways as possible; for example, under the leg or behind the back and try to catch every ball (*Fig 75*).

7 Throw with one hand, catch with two using all the space around the body without moving the feet. Progress to catching with one hand.

8 Throw the ball slightly away from the body and move quickly to catch it with both hands.

9 Move slowly around the playing area, gradually increasing the distance the ball is thrown away from the body, throwing with one hand and catching with the other.

10 Stand approximately 2m from a wall, throw the ball to rebound and catch it using both hands.

11 Throw the ball against a wall and clap or spin before catching it with both hands.

12 Throw the ball against a wall and catch it with the same hand.

13 Throw the ball against a wall with one hand and catch it with the other. Change hands.

14 Throw the ball to bounce off the wall at different heights and angles. Use one or two hands to catch. Progress to aiming at marked targets.

Pairs Practices

1 Players 2m apart, underarm throwing and catching with two hands.

2 As for number 1 but throw to the space above, below and to either side of partner.

3 Move to 5m apart and repeat these exercises.

4 Move to 10m apart, overarm throwing and catching with two hands.

5 Vary the throws to make the partner move in, back or to the side to catch the ball.

6 Standing 2m apart, throw and catch the ball with one hand only.

7 Throw and catch with one hand to the space above, below and to the side of partner.

8 Standing 2m apart, each player has a ball and throws it at the same time, attempting to catch the other ball (*Fig 76*).

Fig 76 In pairs with two balls.

Fig 77 One throws high, one throws low.

9 As above, with one player throwing higher and the other lower (*Fig 77*).

10 Each player has a ball in the right hand and throws it underarm to the partner's left hand. Return the ball with the left hand to partner's right hand.

11 One player holds two balls, one in each hand. Throw one ball to the right and one to the left in quick succession for the partner to catch one-handed. The partner then returns the balls in the same way. Start slowly and then speed up the throws (*Fig 78*).

Fig 78 Quick passing to left and right hand.

12 Standing 2m apart, one player holds two balls, one in each hand. Throw both balls at the same time. The partner attempts to catch one in each hand and returns the balls in the same way (advanced).

13 In pairs, facing a wall at about 2m distance. One player bounces the ball off the wall for the other to catch two-handed.

14 As above, but vary the height, speed and angle of the throw.

15 Throw for the partner to catch using one hand, then the other.

16 One player turns away from the wall, the other throws the ball against it and the first player has to spin round quickly to catch the ball before it bounces.

17 Using one ball only, throw the ball underarm for the other to dive and catch. Use gym mats to land on.

18 Throw alternate high and low short balls to the partner (*Fig 79*).

19 As before, but try to catch the partner out with random throws.

Fig 79 Test partner with long and short throws.

61

20 Throw to a predetermined spot for the partner to catch on the run.

21 Throw overarm to the partner. Each time the ball is caught the receiver steps back 1m. If the ball is dropped, the receiver must move to where it lands. Compete against other pairs to see which finishes the furthest apart.

22 One player holds five balls. The first ball is thrown as far as possible overarm. The partner moves to stand where the ball lands and the thrower then tries to beat that distance with the remaining four throws. The partner moves each time the distance is beaten, thus marking the best throw. Change over after five throws.

23 Players stand approximately 3m apart with a hoop on the ground between them. (This practice is best done on hard ground or indoors.) One player bounces a tennis ball into the hoop, trying to beat the other player with the bounce. The partner tries to catch the ball before it touches the ground a second time, returning the ball in the same way. Start by catching with two hands and progress to one.

Group Practices

Most of the practices for pairs may be also be done in small groups.

1 In threes, make a continuous relay by throwing underarm to the player opposite, then running behind him or her to await the next throw (*Fig 80*).

2 In threes with two balls; one player runs between the posts catching balls thrown overarm alternately by the other two players, 3m from the posts. After catching, the runner stumps the post, throws the ball back to that

Fig 80 Continuous relay.

Fig 81 Running player stumps alternate posts.

feeder and runs across for the next catch. Alternate positions after five throws on each side (*Fig 81*).

3 In threes, form three corners of a square, one player runs to the 'empty corner' each time to catch a ball thrown in that direction (*Fig 82*).

4 In small groups; one player with a bat bowls to him or herself and calls out who is to catch the random hit off the bat. Rotate the batter after ten hits (*Fig 83*).

5 In two groups of three; one forms a triangle and throws and catches around that triangle, counting every catch. At the same time the other team run around the rounders track one at a time. When they have each completed a lap the catching team must stop. Teams then change over and the new catching team attempts to beat their opponents' score.

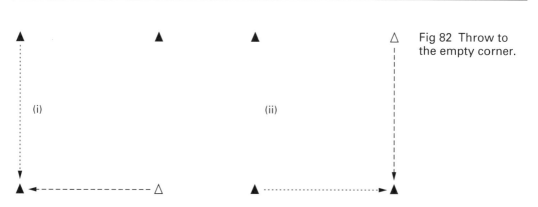

Fig 82 Throw to the empty corner.

6   In threes in a line; two of the players have a ball and throw alternately to the third player in the middle. The middle player must return the ball and spin round to take the next catch as quickly as possible. Rotate after ten throws (*Fig 84*).

7   In fours; players stand in a small restricted area, approximately 5m square, two against two, attempting to keep possession and take five consecutive catches to score a point. Change over when successful.

8   Whole team catching, using ten balls at once. The bowler bowls direct to the backstop who throws on to first post. As soon as the first-post fielder catches the first ball, the bowler bowls

Fig 83 Random catches off the bat.

Fig 84 Middle player turns to take alternate catches.

the next one. As the fielder on each post catches the ball he or she stumps the post and throws to the next fielder. This should be started slowly and then the speed may be increased. If a ball is dropped it should be left out and the exercise carried on without it. This activity may be timed. Fielders may change positions after ten balls (*Fig 85*)

9 Two teams; the bowler bowls in the

usual way and the batter has to run around the posts, whether or not the ball has been hit. The fielding team must return the ball to the first-post fielder who then throws it to second post, and so on to fourth post. The running batter must get to fourth post before the ball and is not allowed to wait at any post. If the batter succeeds in beating the ball to fourth post a rounder is scored. If fourth post is not reached, the batter is out. This is also an excellent throwing practice. Make sure that the fielding team change positions regularly.

10 Circle catching, using four to eight players; throw the ball around the circle as quickly as possible. Add another ball and build up to one ball

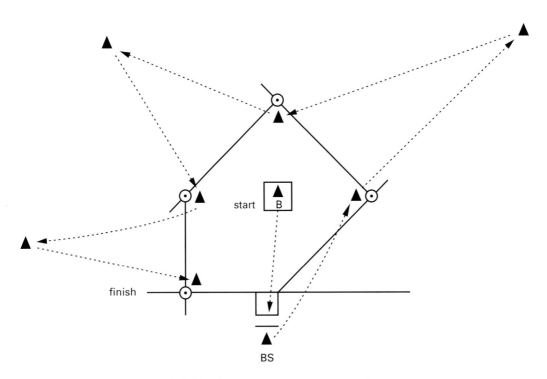

Fig 85 Ball is thrown to each fielder in turn.

Fig 86 Circle catching.

each, with every player throwing and catching at the same time (*Fig 86*).

11 Eight players stand in a circle with one in the middle. The player in the middle throws underarm to each player in turn around the circle. At the same time, another ball is passed around the outside of the circle, so players must watch both balls carefully.

12 Target ball: two teams, each player with a tennis ball, attempt to propel a larger, light ball over the opposition's line by hitting it with the tennis balls. This game works well indoors using a netball court (*Fig 87*).

13 Longball rounders: this game should be played with a soft ball. The playing area may be outside, marked out by cones, or be on a tennis court or in a sports hall. The batters line up behind one line and the fielders space themselves out over the playing area. The bowler stands approximately 8m from the batting line and delivers an underarm ball. The batter attempts to hit the ball and then runs through the fielders to the waiting line. The fielders must throw the ball and hit the running batter below the knee to put him or her out. Fielders must not run with the ball but may throw it to another fielder closer to the batter. Batters may wait at the waiting line for as long as they want and any number of batters may wait there at any one time, but a point cannot be scored unless a player reaches home without

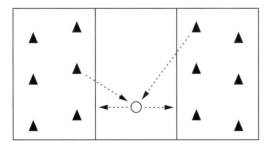

Fig 87 Target ball.

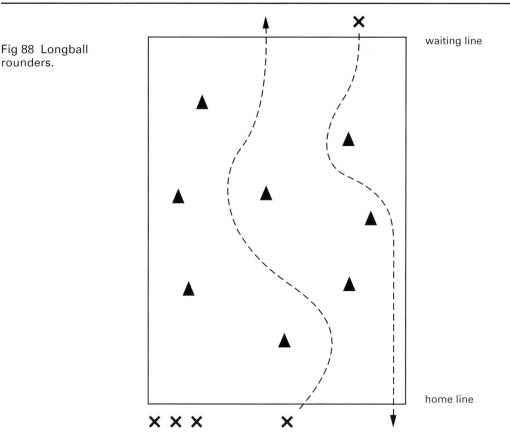

Fig 88 Longball rounders.

waiting line

home line

being hit. Players may be caught out in the usual way (*Fig 88*).

14 Hoop rounders: this game may be played indoors or on a hard surface such as a playground. If playing on grass use hoops to mark the bases; if on concrete or indoors use chalk circles. Use a tennis ball for safety. Bowling and batting areas are marked out and the bowler delivers an underarm ball which is caught by the first batter. That player must then throw the ball as far as possible into the playing area and run around the track, stepping into each circle in turn. The batter is out if:

the ball is caught before it bounces;

the ball is bounced by the fielding team into the circle to which the batter is running;
the ball is thrown backwards; or
the batter runs when the bowler has possession of the ball (*Fig 89*).

15 Hardcourt catch: each team attempts to throw a tennis ball across the opponent's court to a catcher who moves freely in the back court. When the ball is caught the thrower becomes an extra catcher. The first team to get all their players over the back line is the winner. The opposition's ball may be intercepted and thrown, but players must not cross the lines bordering their areas of play (*Fig 90*).

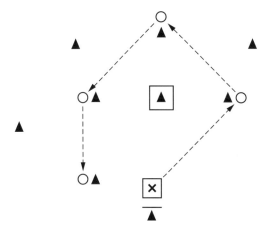

Fig 89 Hoop rounders.

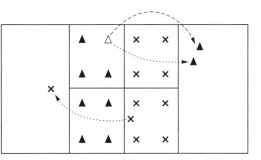

Fig 90 Hardcourt catch.

BATTING PRACTICES

Pairs Practices

1 3m apart: the bowler bowls gently to the bat and the batter just taps the ball back to the bowler.
2 5m apart: the bowler varies the speed, height and angle of delivery; the batter just aims to make contact with the ball.

3 Move to 8m apart: the batter increases the backswing and hits strongly, following through in the direction of the ball.

Group Practices

1 In small groups, each with a bat and ball: bounce the ball gently on the bat, counting the number of bounces; try

Fig 91.

67

Fig 92 Direct the hit.

to beat others in the group (*Fig 91*).

2 In fours with a bowler, batter, back-stop and fielder: the fielder stands between two posts and the batter attempts to strike the ball past the fielder and between the posts; rotate positions after five balls (*Fig 92*).

3 In fours: the fielder moves to stand where the ball stops, but moves only if the distance is increased, thus marking the best hit; the batter tries to improve the hit distance each time; rotate the players.

4 Mini rounders, three teams of three players: rounders played to the usual rules with one team of three batting and the other six players fielding; this activity gives plenty of batting chances and lots of variety as the teams constantly rotate; three posts may be used instead of four.

5 Non-stop rounders, teams of six: the batter must run around the post and return on every good ball; the fielders return the ball to the bowler, who bowls continuously, whether the batter is in place or not; the batter is out if caught by any fielder off the bat or by the backstop directly from the bowler; the batter scores one rounder for each successful circuit of the post; the next batter must rush in to bat when the live batter is out (*Fig 93*).

BOWLING PRACTICES

Individual Practices

1 Throw the ball underarm into plastic hoops or buckets. Score points for different distances or colours (*Fig 94*).

2 Mark a target on a wall approximately 70cm high, 50cm wide and 50cm from the ground. Start close to the wall and bowl to the target, gradually increasing the distance until 7.5m away. Try to get ten consecutive balls into the square. Vary the angle, height and speed of delivery.

3 As above, but divide the rectangle into quarters. Try to aim for one area at a

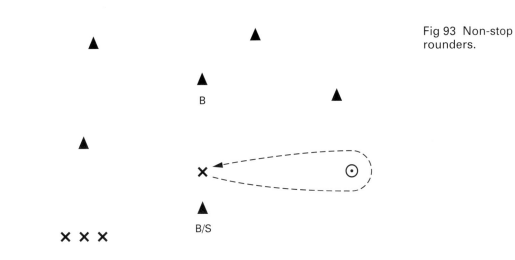

Fig 93 Non-stop rounders.

Fig 94.

time. Increase speed by incorporating a two-step run up.

Pairs Practices

1 Start approximately 3m apart. Bowl underarm to partner, between the top of the head and the knee on the right or the left side.
2 Move to 5m apart. Take a two-step run up before delivering the ball. Increase distance to 7.5m.
3 As above, but partner extends left or right hand. Try to bowl direct to that hand (*Fig 95*).
4 Partner plays as backstop, indicating what type, height and speed of ball to bowl. Experiment with turning the wrist and fingers inwards or outwards as the ball is released to produce spin.

Fig 95 Aim at
partner's hand.

Group Practices

1 In threes: one player bowls, one player holds a hoop close to the body at a level corresponding to the correct bowling area and the third player acts as backstop. The bowler stands about 3m from the hoop and attempts to bowl through it into the backstop's hands, gradually increasing the distance until the correct bowling distance of 7.5m is achieved (*Fig 96*).

2 As above, but with an extra player as batter. Player with the hoop holds it tilted upwards and the bowler must bowl a donkey-drop ball which

Fig 96 Bowl
through the hoop.

Fig 97 Donkey drop practice.

Fig 98 Fast bowling through the hoop.

reaches the batter at the correct height (*Fig 97*).

3 Fast bowling practice in fours with a hoop: bowler starts slowly and gradually increases the speed of delivery (*Fig 98*).

BACKSTOP PRACTICES

Pairs Practices

1 Standing 7.5m apart, one player bowls slow, steady balls and the

71

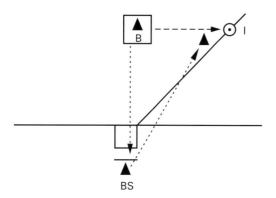

Fig 99 Backstop tries to beat the bowler to first post with the ball.

backstop experiments with different stances.
2 As above, but the bowler should vary the speed, angle and height of delivery.
3 The bowler sends the ball low and to the side so that the backstop has to dive to catch it. A gym mat may be used initially to develop confidence.

4 The bowler takes six balls and bowls them to alternate sides in quick succession.

Group Practices

1 In threes: the bowler bowls direct to the backstop, who practises fast throws to first post. First-post fielder returns the ball to the bowler.
2 As above, but the bowler runs to first post after delivering the ball. Backstop tries to beat the bowler to the post with the ball (*Fig 99*).
3 In fours: the backstop throws to either the first- or the fourth-post fielder who then returns the ball to the bowler. Bowler runs to either post as before.

FIELDING PRACTICES

Individual Practices

1 Roll the ball firmly away, chase it and practise retrieval skills. Pick the ball up with either hand and concentrate on

Fig 100 Retrieving practice.

Fig 101 Stopping the ball on each side.

the correct positioning of the feet (*Fig 100*).

2　As above, but collect the ball, rotate the upper body and throw the ball overarm in the opposite direction. Chase, pick up and repeat.

Pairs Practices

1　Players stand 10m apart and roll the ball to each other to practise stopping, using the gate position on each side (*Fig 101*).

2　As above, but players make each other run hard to either side in order to get behind the ball.

3　Throw the ball underarm so that it bounces, giving a more difficult ball to stop.

4　Stand 10m apart and throw the ball firmly downwards with an overarm action so that it may be caught after one bounce.

5　One player stands between two posts 3m apart. The other stands approximately 8 to 10m away and tries to roll or bounce the ball past the player and between the posts.

Group Practices

1　In threes, with players 10m apart, roll the ball around the triangle, stopping it using the gate position. Vary the speed and direction of the ball to make players work harder.

2　As above, but throw firmly with an overarm action so that the ball bounces once before being caught.

3　In fours: place five balls in the deep

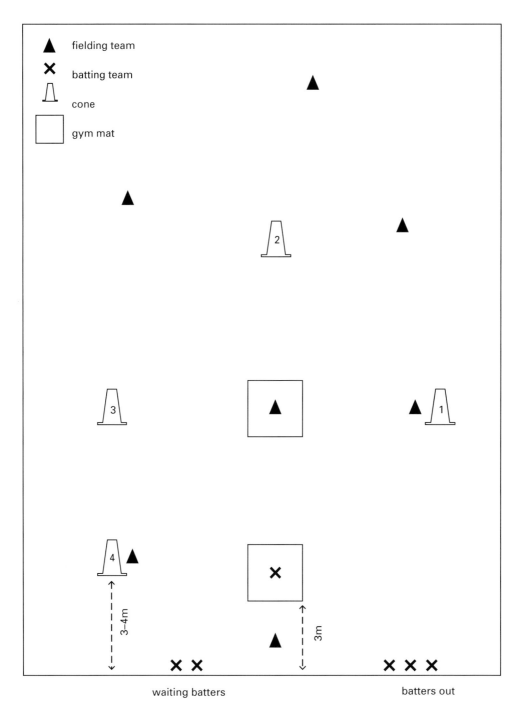

Fig 102 Indoor rounders.

field. Fielder runs to each ball in turn, collecting and throwing to third post, fourth post or the bowler. Time each player.

WHEELCHAIR ROUNDERS

This enjoyable game is played in rehabilitation centres and spinal injury units around the country. Rules may be tailored to suit the needs of the participants and flexibility regarding pitch markings and equipment is essential. To allow for greater speed and mobility, this game is more successful if played indoors or outside on a hard surface such as a playground. The following adaptations may be used:

1 batting and bowling squares are not essential; a chalked cross or cone may mark this area of play;
2 reduce the distance between bowler and batter and reduce the distance between the posts accordingly;
3 post players should remain close to the posts and the bowler should also remain in position; extra fielding players may be added where necessary;
4 to be a good ball, it must be bowled below head height and above the level of the feet; wide and body balls should apply as usual;
5 the batter cannot be stumped out at first post but may not score a rounder if this post is stumped before it is reached;
6 if the game is played outdoors, a backboard is recommended to aid the backstop;
7 'pop' lacrosse sticks or something similar may be used to stop the ball on the ground and to pick it up; they should not be used to catch or throw the ball.

INDOOR ROUNDERS

See *Fig 102*. This fast exciting game may be played in the event of bad weather or used as a training game. It is particularly good as a fielding practice since plenty of catching opportunities always occur. A soft sponge ball, tennis ball or Incrediball should always be used in the interests of safety. Gym mats may be used for the batter and the bowler and the batter's mat should placed at least 3m from the back wall to give the backstop a safe area of play. Cones should be positioned to allow plenty of room around the outside for the running batters. All benches and other obstacles must be removed from the playing area. There should be at least 3m of space after fourth post to allow the batter to slow down safely. Waiting batters and batters out should sit with their backs to the wall at all times.

Rules

Normal NRA rules apply with the following adaptations:
1 teams should be seven a side with a bowler, backstop, first- and fourth-post fielder and three deep fielders;
2 players should be given a number to ensure equal batting opportunities since one catch puts the whole team out (optional).
3 fielders may catch the ball directly off the wall; younger players may be allowed to catch the ball with one hand only, following a bounce;

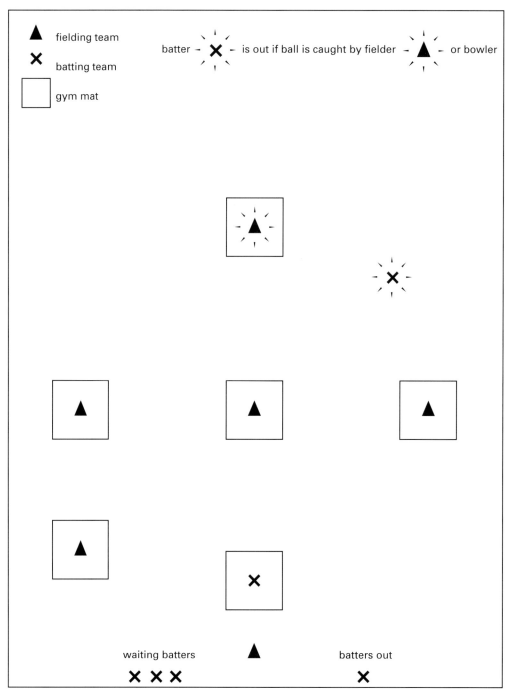

Fig 103 Mat rounders.

4 the bowler must not step off the mat before releasing the ball;

5 the batter must not step off the mat during the batting action.

MAT ROUNDERS

See *Fig 103*. As above, but the post fielders stand on gym mats. To put out a running batter these fielders must simply catch the ball while the batter is between mats. The batter is also out if the player is between mats when the bowler catches the ball from a throw by a fielder.

INCREDIBALL MINI-ROUNDERS

This exciting variation on rounders has been designed by the NRA to attract young players to the game. It involves two teams of four players batting in turn on a smaller version of a rounders pitch. The Incrediball is placed on a batting stand and the batter has to hit the ball into the hitting zone and run as far around the pitch as possible. Rules are simplified and each game lasts for about ten minutes. For more information on this game approach the NRA.

5

Team Play and Tactics

Tactics plays a major part in rounders and a team that is tactically aware may often beat stronger opponents. Here are some tips to improve your team's chances, but remember that the game should take place in the spirit of fair play!

BATTING TEAM

1 Left-handed batters have some advantage in rounders. The field is usually set for a right-handed player and some bowlers find it difficult to bowl to a left-handed batter (*Fig 104*). Left-handed players should not bat consecutively if there are more than one in a team. Alternating right- and left-handed batters disrupts the bowler's rhythm and necessitates frequent field changes (*Figs 105 and 106*).

2 Place the strongest batters first in the batting order. They should then receive more balls in a timed or limited ball innings. Use substitutes carefully to ensure that the best nine hitters bat and the best nine fielders field. Batters may be replaced in the middle of an innings if they are not performing well.

3 Adapt batting styles, taking into

Fig 104 Field placings must be changed for a left-handed batter.

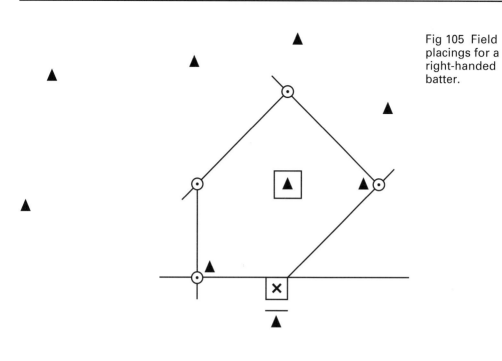

Fig 105 Field placings for a right-handed batter.

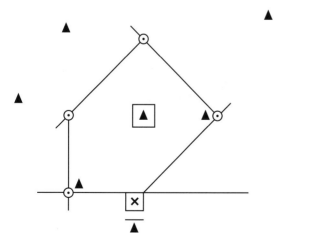

Fig 106 Field placings for a left-handed batter.

account pitch and weather conditions. If the pitch is very rough, a lower hit will bounce and travel unevenly and prove harder to field. If the ball is wet it may be worth taking the risk of a higher hit over the fielders.

4 If only two batters remain, one a strong hitter and the other relatively weak, the weaker one should get him or herself out in order that the stronger player has the choice of three good balls. The fielding team should not want the weaker player out, so it may be necessary to step out of the front of the box while attempting to hit the ball or to run inside first post! These tactics should not be encouraged in children's games but may be used by adult league players.

5 If you have a strong batting team, it would be advisable to field first. The batters would know how many rounders they needed to score and what risks they had to take to achieve the required total.

6 In a match consisting of a limited number of good balls, ask the weaker batters to run when a no ball is bowled. This ensures more balls for the stronger hitters.

7 Make sure that a batter who accidentally drops the bat leaves it and carries on running around the track until the next dead ball situation.

8 Make sure that the opposition *follows on* if they are five or more rounders behind after the first innings.

9 Run on to the next post at every opportunity, unless the post has been stumped and the bowler has the ball. It is better to be at third post rather than cautiously waiting at second since there is always the possibility of an overthrow or fielding error.

10 Disguise backhand hits.

11 A hit to the right involves a much longer distance for the returned ball and more opportunities to score a rounder (*Fig 107*).

12 Communicate with each other while running around the track.

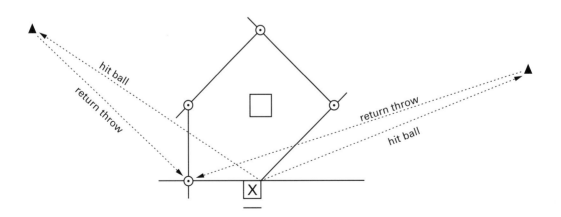

Fig 107 A hit to the right requires a much longer return throw than a hit of the same distance to the left.

FIELDING TEAM

1 Place the best catcher at, or just off, third post. The majority of balls hit in the air by a right-handed batter will travel in this direction.
2 If possible, use a left-handed player at first post. It is easier to stump first post with the left hand after catching the ball. If the backstop throws slightly wide of the post, the ball may be caught more easily with the left hand.
3 Do not attempt to get the weaker batters out in a timed game or in one with a limited number of balls.

4 If a strong batter is waiting at third post, backstop should throw to fourth post rather than first post (*Fig 108*).
5 Use the first-post fielder as an extra deep fielder if the opposing team has a strong left-handed batter who rarely misses the ball or if the last batter is a strong hitter.
6 If the ball is hit into the backward area the backstop should not rush to return the ball since an inaccurate throw into the forward area may allow the batter to run on and score a rounder. Walk the ball to the forward/backward line. This obviously does not apply if there

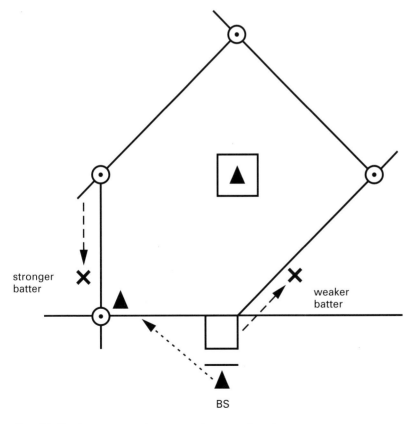

stronger batter

weaker batter

BS

Fig 108 Backstop may choose to throw to fourth post.

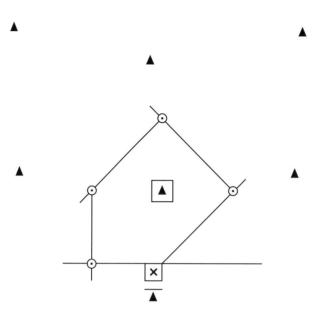

Fig 109 A very defensive field.

Fig 110 Use the full depth of the bowling square.

is another batter on the running track, particularly if that batter needs to get in at fourth post to prolong the innings.

7   Use the fourth-post fielder as an extra deep fielder if playing against a strong batting team. Backstop may take up that position, covered by the first-post fielder or bowler.

8   A strong fielding team might be advised to bat first and defend their score. Fielders may be more motivated with a definite target to defend. A very defensive field should be set for the last few balls of a limited balls innings if strong batters remain in. In some games to prevent rounders may be more important than getting weaker batters out (*Fig 109*).

9   The bowler should practise a quick one–two return pass with the post fielders because many batters are keen to move on to the next post as the fielder returns the ball to the bowler.

10 The bowler should move when necessary to second or third post to catch a returned ball to stump out a batter running to either of these posts. The backstop may move forward to cover a throw to second post and the fourth-post fielder should cover a throw to third post.

11 Vary the bowling constantly to find each batter's weakness. Maximize the space available in the bowling square (*Fig 110*).

12 Practise a quick throw to second post to prevent half a rounder.

END OF THE MATCH

See *Fig 111*. When the last ball of a limited ball or timed game has been bowled, players should be aware that if there is another batter on the track the ball should be held by the bowler in the bowling square until the umpire declares that the innings is over. If there are no waiting batters the ball may be pitched into the batting square before the leading batter touches fourth post. If the live batter runs to first post and another runs from first to second post, merely stumping second post will not prevent the live batter from running on before the ball is returned to the bowler.

This incident occurred in an international match and caused some controversy. The fielding team stumped second post, the batter running to that post was declared out and the fielders started to leave the pitch. The live batter, who had not yet reached first post, continued running and scored a rounder!

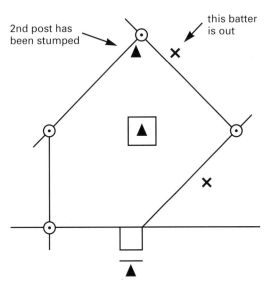

Fig 111 An end of match incident where the live batter has not been put out.

6
Coaching Rounders

The job of the coach is a complex one, demanding good communication and observational skills, the ability to analyse individual and team performances and a knowledge of the correct way to progress and develop skills. A well organized coach should be able to evaluate progress and plan constructive sessions, while motivating and encouraging players to take an active role in the coaching process (*Fig 112*).

OBSERVATION

Good observational skills are essential to a coach as a means of evaluating and analysing performance. Appropriate feedback can then be given to players so that they may improve. In many clubs, schools and colleges the coach may also have to be the umpire and team organizer, but it is nearly impossible to analyse an individual performance while

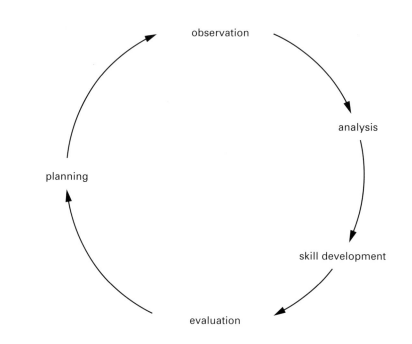

Fig 112.

umpiring and keeping a score sheet. In an ideal situation the coach should not be involved in umpiring and should use reserve players and assistants where necessary to help in recording player and team statistics. The coach must be disciplined enough to observe and analyse in an objective manner. Observation may be distorted in several ways.

Highlighting

It is easy to recall great moments or highlights in a game and it is possible to attribute more success to a player than may be warranted. A batter who hits a really superb shot at the first attempt may achieve little else in the match. How many times do we say that a batter was unlucky to be caught out from the first big hit? A less spectacular player who sneaks around the posts and steals rounders may be more worthy of consideration for future team selection. In the same way a fielder who takes a great catch but fumbles several easier ones may be a less valuable team member than a steady fourth-post fielder who makes only one vital error but unluckily concedes a rounder.

Personal Bias

This may sometimes become evident when teachers coach the same group for several sports. It is natural to assume and is often, though not always, true, that a player who is superb at one sport may excel at all others too and many school rounders teams are made up of the previous term's netball or hockey team players. It is worth remembering that the player who avoids winter games, preferring to have indoor tennis lessons, may well transfer those tennis skills successfully to rounders. A young player's confidence may really suffer if the coach shows favouritism in selection. All the players should be given the same opportunities in all positions during lesson time. Once a potential team has emerged team practice time may be used to develop positional players according to their abilities.

Memory

Coaches may improve their memory and recall in many ways. Remaining calm during a match by avoiding involvement on an emotional level will help their later recollection of performance since a single, controversial incident or confrontation may easily affect memory and judgement. Concentrating on only one aspect of play during an innings, for example, running between the posts or movement of the deep fielders, should provide material for future coaching sessions. The use of video recording is becoming common in all sports. Careful positioning will ensure that a worthwhile recording is made. Players can see their own technique and performance and the coach has replayable footage of incidents that could have been forgotten in the post-match analysis. Many coaches also take notes or use tape-recording equipment during matches to aid their recall.

PERFORMANCE ANALYSIS

The analysis of players during both training sessions and matches may produce startling differences. Match situations produce tension which affects players in different ways. Walking into the batting square when all eyes are focused on it may reduce a player to jelly! Some players see the opportunity as an ordeal, particularly if they are the last batter in. Others rise to the challenge.

The comparative analysis of players should occur in the same game situation. Performing under pressure is an essential requirement at all levels of sport. Some players never seem to perform well when it really matters and much research has been done on the psychological aspects of performance.

Analysis is not only about the identification of faults. Coaching should be a positive process, emphasizing the players' strengths and building confidence by highlighting these features. Analysis charts should contain positive as well as negative information and when discussing individual performances, a good coach will point out successes before discussing faults (*Figs 113 to 117*).

SKILL DEVELOPMENT

Successful analysis will provide material for the continual development of skills. Simple skills may be learned as a whole, but more complicated ones can be broken down, practised in parts and then put back together again.

Introducing a New Skill

1 Explain the skill so that players may understand what they are trying to do.
2 Allow players to try out the skill first. This gives the coach some idea of ability levels. If a player is allowed to try out a new technique and fails to master it, that player will be more receptive to coaching.
3 Use a good player to demonstrate the skill correctly.
4 Allow time to practise and assist individuals with the technique, breaking the skill down if necessary.
5 Let players apply the skill in a game situation.

EVALUATION

This should be a continual process and the resulting information will determine the next stage of coaching. A good coach should ask players to evaluate their own performances and contribute thoughts and ideas in training sessions.

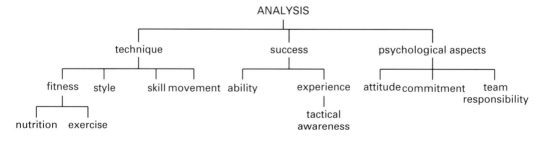

Fig 113 Some factors for consideration in analysis.

BATTER

POSITIONING AND STANCE	STRIKE	PROGRESSION	HOW OUT
GOOD POOR	HIT MISS	1st POST	STEPPED OUT
		2nd POST	CAUGHT
		3rd POST	Caught by B/S Bow. Post Field.
Forehand	**HEIGHT** HIGH MED. LOW	4th POST	STUMPED AT 1st 2nd 3rd 4th box
Backhand			
Disguised	**DIRECTION** Behind Bowler	**ROUNDERS SCORED**	LOST CONTACT
TIMING	Between F/B line and 1st post		OVERTOOK
Good Poor	1st Deep 3rd Deep		**ORDER WHEN OUT**
	2nd Deep 4th Deep		

Fig 114 Analysis of batter's performance.

BOWLER

DELIVERY		CATCHES			COVER	
		OFF BAT			GOOD	POOR
Good Ball	No Ball	Caught	Dropped			
HIT	MISSED	FROM FIELDER			Appropriate	Slow
High	Low	Caught	Dropped			Wrong Decision
Fast	Wide					
Slow	Body					
Donkey Drop	Spin	Penalty 1/2 rounders				
					Notes:	

Fig 115 Analysis of bowler's performance.

BACKSTOP

POSITIONING				COVERING		
GOOD	POOR			GOOD	POOR	
					Slow	
	Penalty 1/2 rounders				Wrong Decision	

THROWS TO 1st POST		
Accurate	Inaccurate
Appropriate	Inappropriate

CATCHES OFF BAT

TO BOWLER		
Caught	Dropped
Accurate	Inaccurate
Appropriate	Inappropriate

CATCHES OFF BOWLING

TO A POST		
Caught	Dropped
Accurate	Inaccurate
Appropriate	Inappropriate

DECISION MAKING

Appropriate	Inappropriate
Batter out/stopped	

Notes:

Fig 116 Analysis of backstop's performance.

FIELDER

POSITIONING		THROWS TO 1ST POST		COVERING	
Good	Poor	Accurate	Inaccurate	Good	Poor
					wrong decision

MOVEMENT					
Good	Poor	Appropriate	Inappropriate		

CATCHES		TO BOWLER		NOTES
Caught	Dropped	Accurate	Inaccurate	

DECISION MAKING			
Appropriate	Inappropriate	Appropriate	Inappropriate

Fig 117 Analysis of a fielder's performance.

Skill	Fault	Cause	Correction
BATTING	Missing the ball	Taking eye off the ball before moment of contact	Decide where to hit before taking up position and watch ball on to the bat
	Short hit	1. Striking downwards at the ball	Adjust starting position, keep bat parallel during swing and follow through upwards
		2. Using elbow and not shoulder during the swing	Start with arm extended in ready position
		3. Not stepping into swing and failing to transfer weight through the lower body	Practise swing and transfer of weight without a ball
	Repeatedly being caught	Striking the ball upwards	Try to take donkey drop or slow balls early, before they reach knee height
BOWLING	Delivery too high	1. Remaining upright as the ball is released	Bend knees as arm is swung through
		2. Late release of the ball	Release the ball at the lowest point of the swing
	Delivery too low	1. Insufficient power	a) Run up to increase speed b) Increase backswing
		2. Early release of the ball	Release the ball on the upward swing
	Delivery too wide	1. Standing too square on release of the ball	Adjust position, pointing shoulder of non-bowling arm towards the batter
		2. Bowling from the front left corner of the bowling square	Change angle of delivery by releasing the ball from the front centre or right corner of the bowling square
	Body ball	1. Standing at too acute an angle to the batter	Adjust position in square
		2. Bowling from the front right hand corner of the bowling square	Change angle of delivery by moving to the left

Fig 118 Common faults and corrections (depicted in Figs 119–123).

Skill	Fault	Cause	Correction
1st POST FIELDING	Slow to stump the post	Having to adjust body position in relation to the post after the ball has been caught	Stand at an arm's length from the post, so catch and stumping can be performed in one movement
4th POST FIELDING	Out of position for the throw	Creeping forward towards the fielder to shorten the throwing distance	Stay close to the post. Utilise other fielders if the return throw is short
DEEP FIELDING	Failure to stop a low ball	1. Moving too slowly to get behind the ball	Stay alert and walk in towards the pitch
		2. Not using the body as a block	Adopt the gate position

Fig 118 *(continued)*

Fig 119 Taking eyes off the ball.

Fig 120 Hitting downwards at the ball.

Fig 121 Using elbow and not the shoulder.

PLANNING

The planning of training sessions is an essential part of the coaching process. The coach should use all the information available to set appropriate and achievable goals. It is unwise to plan too far ahead. Certain sessions may need to be repeated or reworked and flexibility within a structured approach is necessary. To concentrate on one skill for a number of sessions may result in the deterioration of another, so the coaching programme should include previously learned skills alongside new ones. Coaching sessions will vary but should include the following:

1 discussion of aims;
2 warm up;
3 introductory activity;
4 skills;
5 progression of skills into a modified or full game;
6 cool down and session review.

Fig 122 Not stepping into the hit.

Fig123 Standing too close to the post.

7
Rules Clinic

Rounders is a complicated game and many regions have their own, local rules. The NRA is encouraging players to adhere to the national rules as they appear in its publication *Rules of the Game of Rounders and Hints to Umpires*. Some of the more common problems that arise are discussed in this chapter.

BATTING

Q. Am I allowed to step out of the batting square while attempting to hit the ball? (*Figs 124–126*)

A. If a good ball is bowled you may step out at either side of the square but not out of the front or the back. If a no-ball is bowled then you may step out of the square in any direction. Once the ball has been struck or missed, then you may leave the square in any direction.

Q. Can I score on a no ball?

A. Yes, you may score in the usual ways.

Q. Can I be out on a no ball?

A. Not by stepping out of the batting square; not by being caught; not by being stumped at first post. Once you are passed first post, all other infringements apply.

Q. Do I have to run on a no ball?

A. No, you have a choice, but if you run to within reach of first post the umpire will rule that you have 'taken' the ball.

Q. May I run on a *backward hit*?

A. Only to first post until the ball is returned to the forward area, then you may carry on running around the posts. The umpire will ask you to return to first post if you fail to comply with this rule.

Q. What if I drop my bat?

Fig 124 Batter out.

Fig 125 Batter out.

Fig 126 Batter not out.

A. If you are judged to have thrown it deliberately then you will be out. If it is accidental, continue around the posts without it and it will be returned to you at the next dead ball situation.

Q. What happens if I lose contact with a post?

A. If the bowler has the ball within the bowling square or is in the process of bowling, you will be out. If the bowler does not have the ball and you are

Fig127 The safest way to maintain contact with the post.

Fig 129 If the batter loses contact with the post while the bowler has the ball, she will be out.

Fig128 This is more risky as contact may be lost.

between posts the umpire will order you on to the next post and you may be put out in the usual ways (*Figs 127 to 129*).

Q. What if I run inside the posts? (*Fig 130*)

A. You will be out unless you are forced to do so by the fielding team. If this is the case you will be awarded a penalty half rounder (*Fig 131*).

Q. What happens if the batter in front of me is too slow and I overtake? (*Fig 132*)

A. You will be out. If two batters are waiting at the same post the umpire

Fig 130 Batter is out for running inside the post.

will order the first one to run on and that player may be stumped at the next post.

Q. Does it matter if I forget to touch fourth post?

A. Yes! This causes all sorts of problems: if a fielder touches fourth post with the ball before you do you will be out. If the fielding team fail to notice and return the ball to the bowler who then

Fig 131 A batter forced inside the track will be awarded a penalty half rounder.

Fig 132 Do not overtake.

bowls the next ball, then you have got away with it. If you are the live batter this also applies and you cannot score a rounder unless you touch fourth post before the next ball is bowled (*Fig 133*).

Q. What happens if the batter in front of me does not touch fourth post, I do touch fourth post and a fielder then stumps the post?

A. You will be out for overtaking. The previous batter is stumped out.

Q. If the ball hits me as I am running around the track, is this obstruction?

Fig 133 Touching fourth post is essential.

Fig 134 No ball; bowler has stepped out over the front line during the bowling action.

Fig 135 No ball; bowler's foot is in the air but over the line.

A. Not unless you deliberately deflect the ball, in which case you will be out.

Q. How can the fielders stop me from scoring a rounder?

A. In three ways:
   1. By putting you out.
   2. By stumping the post ahead of the one you have reached or are within reach of. If you have reached first

post they must stump second. If you have reached second post they must stump third. If you have reached third post they must stump fourth. This rule often causes confusion. You cannot be out if the post ahead of you is stumped provided that you have not left the post you are at. As the ball is returned to the

Fig 136 Spin bowling is allowed.

bowler or thrown to another fielder you may run on, but you cannot score. Stumping fourth post if you are not yet within reach of third post has no purpose whatsoever.

3. By throwing the ball to the bowler who maintains possession in the bowling square before you reach third post.

Q. Can I score a rounder if I don't hit the ball?

A. No, you may score only half a rounder if you manage to get all the way round as the live batter.

Q. Can I go back to a post?

A. No, unless you are ordered to do so by the umpire.

Q. If I am waiting at a post and the bowler

Fig137 Batter may run on.

Fig 138 Batter may run on.

Fig 139 Batter must wait at the post.

bowls a no ball to the next batter, do I have to run?

A. No. You have a choice, unless another batter runs to your post in which case you must run on. Even if the bowler bowls a good ball you do not have to run on unless someone is running to your post.

Q. What happens if I am the live batter and I get to fourth post but another batter causes an obstruction?

A. The other batter is out. You are in, but your rounder does not count.

Q. If I am obstructed after touching fourth post will I be awarded a penalty half rounder?

A. No, you cannot be obstructed after touching fourth post. If you miss the

Fig 141 A dummy bowl is not allowed.

Fig 140 A good tactic is to bowl close to the body.

post and attempt to run back to touch it, you may then be obstructed by the fielders.

Q. What happens if I am the only batter left in?

A. You have the option of three good balls. If the ball is caught from any of these you are out. If you run to within reach of, make contact with or run past first post, the umpire will rule that you have taken that ball. Each time you score a rounder, or half a rounder if you get round without hitting the ball, you are entitled to a rest of one minute before the next set of three balls.

Q. What happens if the backstop steps forward over the 1m backstop line before I have tried to hit the ball?

A. You will be awarded a penalty half rounder for obstruction in addition to any rounder or half rounder you may subsequently score. If this occurs you may not be stumped out at first post.

103

Fig 142
Obstruction by a
batter deviating
from the running
track.

BOWLING

Q. May I take a run up before bowling?

A. Yes, but you must be within the bowler's square as you start. If you walk into the bowling square holding the ball then there must be a deliberate break before you start to bowl.

Q. May I step out of the front of the square as I release the ball? (*Fig 134*)

A. No. You must have released the ball before you step out of the square.

Q. May my foot be over the front line of

Fig 143 Batter is
out when the post
ahead is stumped.

Fig 144 Post may be stumped by the ball held in the hand.

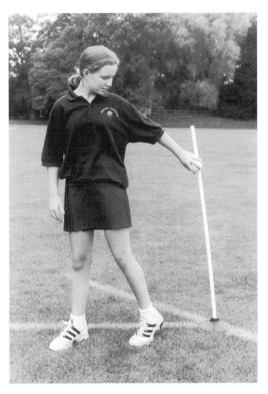

Fig 145 Post may also be stumped by the hand holding the ball.

the square if it is in the air? (*Fig 135*)

A. No.

Q. If I bowl a no ball, may I be replaced by another bowler?

A. Yes, but your no ball will still stand, and if your replacement bowls a consecutive no ball, then half a rounder will be awarded to the batting team.

Q. May I spin the ball? (*Fig 136*)

A. Yes, provided that the delivery is underarm and in a smooth and continuous action.

Q. If the batter holds the bat in the middle of the body, may I bowl to the middle too?

A. No. The batter must indicate to which side he or she wants you to bowl to.

Q. If the ball is returned to me but I drop it in my square, what happens?

A. The batters may run on until you are holding the ball, with both feet in the bowler's square (*Figs 137 to 139*).

Q. The batter is very small and my bowling keeps going over her head height, but it is my normal height of delivery. Why is the umpire calling no balls?

A. You must adjust your bowling according to the height of the individual batter.

Fig 146 If the post is dislodged, stump the base; if that has moved, stump the pitch marking.

Fig 147 Stumping batting square before the last batter reaches fourth post.

Q. May I bowl as close to the body as I can? (*Fig 140*)

A. Yes. This is an excellent bowling technique provided that, in the umpire's opinion, the ball would not strike the batter,

Q. How wide may I bowl the ball?

A. Provided that you bowl to the side indicated by the batter, you may bowl as wide as the player can reach with an outstretched bat. This is often further than you imagine.

Q. If fourth post is stumped and I walk with the ball back to my square, may

Fig 148 Waiting batters obstruct fielders.

the batter run on from third post?

A. Yes, but a rounder would not be scored by that batter. A batter would not normally take this risk, however, as you could return the ball quickly to the fourth-post fielder.

Q. May I pretend to bowl but not release the ball in order to get the batters to leave their posts? (*Fig 141*)

A. No, a *dummy ball* is not allowed. If you do this the umpire will return the batters to their posts and ask you to bowl again.

Q. May I wear gloves to bowl?

A. Yes, any player may wear gloves.

FIELDING

Q. If I accidentally obstruct the batter as she is running around the track, will I give away a penalty half rounder?

A. Yes. There is no such thing as accidental obstruction. You must give right of way to the running batter on the track. If you force the batter to run inside the track she will not be given out.

Q. May I be obstructed by a batter? (*Fig 142*)

A. Yes. A batter who deviates from the running track and impedes your collection of the ball will be given out.

Q. How do I stump a batter out?

A. You must touch the post immediately ahead of the batter (*Fig 143*). This may be done with the ball held in the hand or with the hand holding the ball (*Figs 144 and 145*).

Q. What do I do if the post has been knocked down or removed? (*Fig 146*)

A. Stump the base if it is still in its correct position. If not, touch the white mark where that base and post usually stand. This also applies to the batting team.

Q. Can the fielding team get more than one batter out at once?

A. Yes. You should always be aiming for this. The second-post fielder may catch out the live batter, stump out the previous batter running to that post and then throw to the fourth-post fielder who stumps out another batter running from third to fourth post!

Q. Why do so many fielding teams stump fourth post then return the ball to the bowler when there is no one at third post?

A. I don't know! This has no purpose at all because the live batter who is not yet at third may run on as the ball is being returned and score in the usual way.

Q. How can a fielder put the whole batting side out?

A. If there are no waiting batters, the fielder must pitch the ball into the batting square before the leading batter on the track reaches and touches fourth post (*Fig 147*). Alternatively, the ball may be returned to the bowler before that batter reaches third post.

Q. Can I get a player out by touching her on the back with the ball as she runs past me?

A. No. This rule was changed years ago.

Q. If I am injured or not playing well may I be substituted?

A. Yes. Any batter or fielder from the maximum fifteen named players may be substituted at a dead ball situation. Once substituted, a fielder may return to the game provided that there are no more than nine players on the field at any one time. A batter must return to the position of their original number. The minimum number of players required in a team is six.

Q. If the players waiting to bat prevent me from fielding the ball, what happens? (*Fig 148*)

A. You will be awarded a penalty half rounder for obstruction.

8
Fitness for Rounders

In order to really enjoy playing rounders, it is advisable to achieve a high level of fitness. This is essential for advanced players, where performance must be sustained throughout the game. Fitness not only improves performance it also helps to prevent injury, reduce mental and physical fatigue, and ensure a consistently high level of skill under pressure. Training for sport also has a positive effect over the rest of a player's life, with improved general health and well being.

PHYSICAL FITNESS

Physical fitness is the overall physical condition of a player and there are wide variations between individuals. The following general principles affect fitness and the coach should have a good understanding of these:

1 Overload
2 Adaptation
3 Progression
4 Specificity
5 Reversibility
6 Variation
7 Recovery.

Overload

This is essential for training to have an effect. The body responds well to unusual physical demand but overload must be progressive to avoid damage to its systems.

Adaptation

As training progresses, the body quickly adapts to the demands made on it. Increased muscle strength and heart function may result in a reduced effect from the exercise programme. The body must be given time to adapt to each new level of fitness before the next progression is made.

Progression

There are many ways of progressing in a fitness programme. Increased repetitions, the use of greater weight or a higher intensity of exercise can produce a gradual improvement in endurance, strength and cardiovascular efficiency.

Specificity

Training should be specific to the sport coached. In rounders, for example, speed training should include cornering to simulate running around the track. Within each sport, individuals should undergo training specific to their own positional requirements.

Reversibility

A falling off in fitness quickly occurs if training stops. Once the optimum level of fitness is achieved, maintenance training will be required to prevent this decline.

Variation

Factors such as general health, body shape, maturity and hereditary differences may affect the outcome of training.

Individuals may also have a different mental approach to physical activity. All these factors will affect progression and regular assessment is essential. Variation in training programmes will help to maintain motivation and enthusiasm and prevent boredom.

Recovery

This is often neglected in fitness programmes. Appropriate rest periods

Fig 149 Rounders requires a good deal of strength.

should be incorporated into training sessions. Recovery from injury may be active, involving low intensity exercises or massage, or passive, involving complete rest.

THE COMPONENTS OF PHYSICAL FITNESS

The prime ones are:

1 Strength/power
2 Endurance
3 Flexibility
4 Speed/speed of reaction

To these components we must add skill, psychological factors and nutritional preparation, all essential when aiming to achieve optimum performance levels.

Strength/power

Strength is important in rounders, producing the power required for sprinting, hitting and throwing (*Fig 149*). Improved muscle strength is achieved by applying a resistance to a muscle or group of muscles and training them to cope with a heightened load.

Strength may be increased in several ways:

a) Through other sports: playing a variety of other sports such as netball, basketball or tennis will improve arm and leg strength.
b) Weight training: great care should be taken with weight training and programmes must be planned using expert advice. Imbalance and damage to muscles may result from the inappropriate use of weights. Children

should not train with weights to increase strength since they may be vulnerable to injury. Exercises using the child's own body weight as resistance will prevent this.
c) Circuits: these are suitable for all age groups and produce a balanced work out if correctly planned. Activities using the same muscle or group of muscles should not run consecutively in order to allow adequate rest time. Activities may be timed and the number of repetitions of each exercise recorded to ensure that progress is being made. A regular check on technique should ensure that the exercises are being performed correctly (*Fig 150*).

Endurance

Rounders players need endurance in order to cope with repeated running around the track under pressure. This is particularly true when a team has only two players left in. Those players may run several circuits at full speed with little recovery time. Endurance may be aerobic, anaerobic or muscular. During *aerobic* exercise the body uses oxygen to help to produce enough energy to maintain muscular effort for long periods. A healthy heart/lung function is essential in order to deliver this oxygen efficiently. This may be achieved by regular continuous exercise, perhaps involving swimming, running or cycling for periods of around twenty minutes at a time. Endurance circuits consisting of exercises such as skipping, jogging or jumping may also improve aerobic fitness. *Anaerobic* endurance involves an element of speed and is the body's ability to sustain short periods of intense

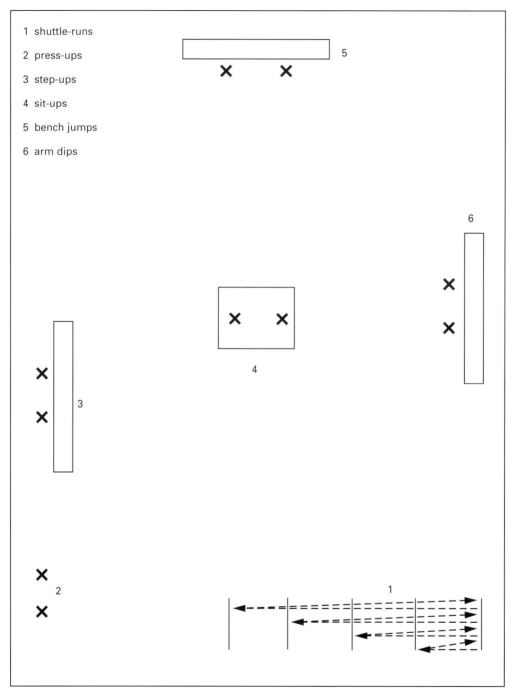

Fig 150 Strength circuit.

Fig 151 A sudden dynamic movement may lead to injury.

Fig 152 Calf stretch.

activity; for example, accelerating between third and fourth posts to score a rounder. Energy for this is supplied by fuel stored in the muscles and there is no demand for extra oxygen. Anaerobic endurance may be improved by interval training where high intensity exercise is interspersed with lighter exercise or rest, and circuit training involving activities performed at speed, for example, timed shuttle running. *Muscular* endurance is the capacity of a group of muscles to sustain activity throughout the exercise period. The bowler requires muscular endurance in order to deliver an accurate ball repeatedly, and the backstop utilises a different group of muscles to throw to the first-post fielder. Progressive training involving increased repetitions to the appropriate muscle groups will increase muscular endurance. This may be achieved through weight training, using low weights with a gradual increase in repetitions and specifically designed circuits.

113

Fig 153 Shoulder stretch.

Flexibility

Flexibility is essential to enable full movement around joints or groups of joints. Limited flexibility may lead to poor techniques when performing a skill and injury to unstretched muscles during sudden dynamic movements (*Fig 151*). The range of movement around joints may be improved considerably by gradual stretching. This will lead to better technique and more efficient use of energy, but the muscles must be strong enough to support the joints and so strength must also be developed. Too much strength training may limit the potential flexibility of the joint so it is important that a balance be achieved. Stretching should form a part of every warm-up and cooldown routine. The body temperature must be raised before stretching. This may be achieved by gentle jogging activities using the large muscle groups. The safest type of stretch is an active one

Fig 154 Back stretch.

Fig 155 Hamstring stretch.

performed individually since passive stretching may result in damage around the joint. For a warm-up the stretch should be held for about ten seconds and, if tension in the muscle increases, the exercise should be stopped. Players should be encouraged to perform stretches in a full tracksuit and with the body in a warm and relaxed state. Stretches to improve the range of movement should be held for between ten to twenty seconds and the joint should not be forced or held in an uncomfortable position (*Figs 152 to 156*).

Speed

Speed is essential at all levels of rounders. Many players with strong hits are let down by their running speed and never seem to make it past third post. They would do well to concentrate on training to improve this part of their game. (*Fig 157*). Within a training programme speed activities may be

Fig 156 Quadriceps stretch.

Fig 157 Speed around the running track.

incorporated in circuits designed around short sprints, pressure speed (timed) drills and reflex activities. Players should work to their maximum during speed work so adequate periods of rest between activities are important. Increasing leg strength will also help to improve speed, especially in leaving the batting square and changing direction around the posts. This may be achieved by playing other

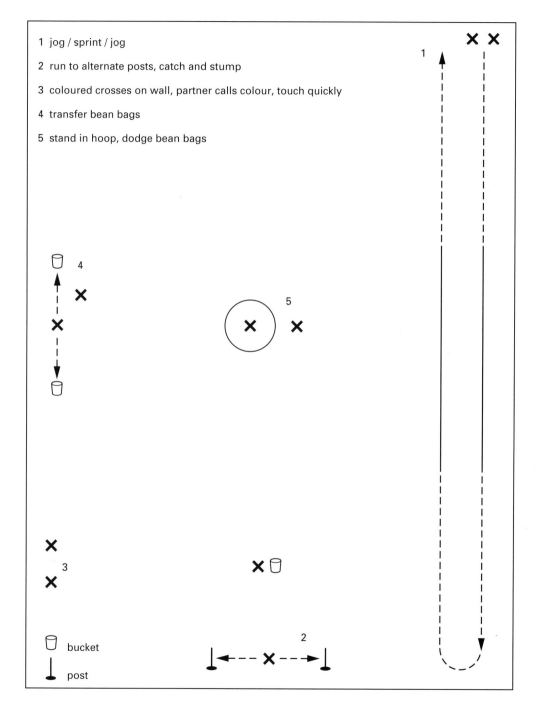

Fig 158 Speed and reaction circuit.

Fig 159 Rounders activity circuit for children.

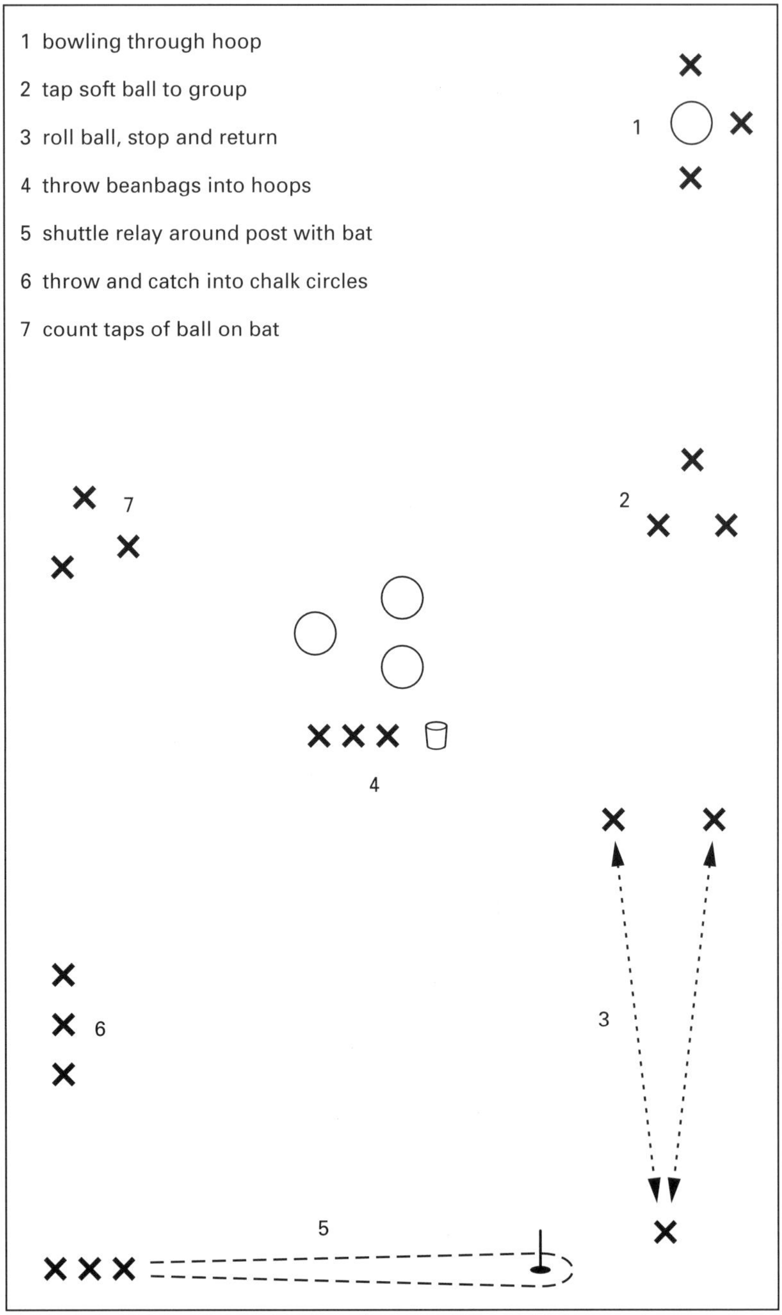
1 bowling through hoop
2 tap soft ball to group
3 roll ball, stop and return
4 throw beanbags into hoops
5 shuttle relay around post with bat
6 throw and catch into chalk circles
7 count taps of ball on bat
1
7
2
4
3
6
5

games involving bursts of acceleration, for example, netball and hockey (*Fig 158*).

Nutrition

Energy from food, drink and oxygen is converted by the body into active energy for sport. Players must ensure that they take in enough energy to meet their requirements by drinking plenty of fluids before, during and after a match or training session and they should eat a meal high in carbohydrates (such as pasta, rice or bread) at least two hours before a match. After a game or training session, food and drink supplies must be replaced as quickly as possible, while metabolism is still high. All players who eat a healthy diet as part of their training programme will ensure that they get the maximum benefit and enjoyment from their sport.

Glossary

Backhand hit A deceptive shot to the right by a right-handed player hitting across the body.

Backstop The fielder who stands behind the batter to catch, stop or retrieve the ball (*Fig 160*).

Backstop line A line 1m behind the back line of the batting square, behind which the backstop must stand until the batter has attempted a hit.

Backward area The area behind the forward/backward line and the imaginary continuation of it.

Backward hit A ball which, when struck, pitches in the backward area. This does not refer to a ball that drops in the forward area and afterwards goes behind.

Batting order The numbered order of players coming in to bat as submitted to the umpire. This must be adhered to unless players are out or substituted.

Fig 160 Backstop.

Fig 161 Batting square.

Batting square An area 2m square within which the batter must stand with both feet while awaiting the ball (*Fig 161*).

Body ball A ball which, in the opinion of the umpire, would have hit the batter. If the batter moves into a position where the ball makes contact with the body after the ball is released a no ball should not be called.

Boundary line In certain competitions this line is marked in the outfield and any ball which is hit by the batter and crosses

Fig 162 Bowling square.

121

Fig 163 Dynamic throwing position.

the line, either on the ground or in the air, will count as a rounder. Fielders must keep the whole of the both feet inside the line to prevent a rounder from being scored.

Bowling square   An area 2.5m square within which the bowler must remain with both feet until the ball is released (*Fig 162*).

Calling in   A batter must not step into the batting square until called in by name or number by the batter's umpire.

Dead ball   A time in the game when play has stopped for some reason such as substitution.

Deep fielder   A player who fields from a position away from the posts and outside the running track.

Donkey drop   A ball which appears to be travelling too high but drops at the last minute to become a good ball.

Dummy bowl   When the bowler deliberately stops in mid action in an attempt to cause the batters to lose contact with their posts. This is not allowed and if it happens players will be allowed to return to their positions.

Dynamic throwing position   The correct position for the most effective and efficient return of the ball (*Fig 163*).

Follow on   If a team is five or more rounders behind after the first innings.

Forward area   The front line of the batting square is extended in both directions by solid lines measuring at least 12m in length. This line, the imaginary continuation of it and the area in front of it comprise the forward area.

Forward/backward line   The line between the forward and the backward area, forming part of the forward area.

Gate position   A method of stopping the ball using the lower body and hands to form a barrier (*Fig 164*).

Giving in   Absorbing the speed of the ball as it is caught.

Good ball   A ball delivered by the bowler in accordance with the rules. Each batter is entitled to only one good ball (*Fig 165*).

Half a rounder   Scored by the batter if the player completes the track, fulfilling

Fig 164 Gate position.

the same conditions as for scoring a rounder but without hitting the ball. It is also scored if the live batter reaches second post and is not subsequently put out at third or fourth post.

Hand   The NRA definition is: from the tips of the fingers to the joint of the wrist and forearm.

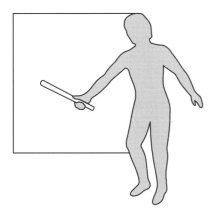

Fig 165 Good ball area.

Incrediball   A softer rounders ball, ideal for use by children.

Innings   The period when a team bats. Normally each team would have two innings in a match.

Last batter   The only batter left in on entering the square. The last batter has the choice of three good balls. If the player is caught from any of these balls, however, he or she will be out. After each rounder scored the player is entitled to a rest of one minute before the next set of three good balls.

Line for batters out   A line drawn 10m behind the front of the batting square on the right side of the pitch, behind which the batters who are out must stand.

Line for waiting batters   A line drawn 10m behind the front of the batting square on the left side of the pitch, behind which the waiting batters must stand.

Live batter   The batter to whom the most recent ball was bowled, irrespective of whether the ball was a good ball or a no ball.

123

Fig 166 Running track.

No ball A ball delivered by the bowler which, in the opinion of the umpire, infringes one or more of the rules.

Obstruction Impeding, verbally misleading or preventing the opposition from catching, fielding, running or throwing the ball during the course of the game. Both fielders and batters may be guilty of obstruction.

Penalty half rounder Awarded to the batting team following certain infringements by the fielding side. One or more

Fig 167 2m line (post extension line).

may be awarded in addition to a rounder or half a rounder scored in the usual way. The fielding team may be awarded a penalty half rounder if they are obstructed by the waiting batters.

Rounder If, after hitting the ball, the batter succeeds in running around the posts and touches fourth post before the next ball is bowled, without infringing any rule, then a rounder is awarded.

Running track The course normally taken by batters around the posts (*Fig 166*).

Side out When there are no waiting batters, all the batters on the running track may be put out simultaneously when a fielder pitches or places the ball into the batting square before the leading batter has reached and touched fourth post. Side out also occurs where there is no batter waiting to bat and the bowler has possession of the ball in the bowling square.

Stumped out Being put out by a fielder touching the post to which the batter is running with the ball held in the hand or the hand holding the ball.

Wide ball A ball which passes outside the normal reach of the batter. A ball bowled outside the square is not necessarily a wide.

2m line Extension lines drawn at the posts to assist the umpires when deciding whether a batter has overrun the post or has turned and set off for the next post (*Fig 167*).

Index